JOHN BETJEMAN
MAKING LIGHT

JOHN BETJEMAN
MAKING LIGHT

TIM HANCOCK

Greenwich Exchange
London

Greenwich Exchange, London

First published in Great Britain in 2021
All rights reserved

John Betjeman: Making Light
© Tim Hancock, 2021

Printed and bound by imprintdigital.com
Cover design by December Publications
Tel: 07951511275

Greenwich Exchange Website: www.greenex.co.uk

Cataloguing in Publication Data is available
from the British Library

Cover: Sir John Betjeman by Ian Dickson
(reproduced courtesy of Getty Images)

ISBN: 978-1-910996-57-7

to Helen

CONTENTS

PREFACE AND ACKNOWLEDGEMENTS

THOUGH BLESSED WITH A DEVOTED BIOGRAPHER (Bevis Hillier) and a conscientious correspondence editor (his daughter, Candida Lycett Green), John Betjeman has not been well served by the critics. The contempt and neglect that he anticipated from this quarter came to pass, but even appreciative readers have felt the need to apologise for his poetry, and struggled to catch its idiosyncratic spirit. One of the problems, I think, has been a general tendency to view Betjeman's poems primarily in literary and cultural contexts rather than that of his life. Book-lover, rail-rider, church-crawler he may have been, but John Betjeman was not permanently lost in contemplation of some obscure volume, branch-line, or architectural detail left over from the Victorian age. He was an emotional man whose best poems were stimulated less by art and history than by feelings and relationships. Thanks to the efforts of Hillier and Lycett Green we now know an awful lot about his life, and as time passes and sensitivities fade secrets that were once closely guarded have become common knowledge.

This reconsideration of his poetry was written in the belief that such biographical information now needs to be mapped onto Betjeman's stanzas. 'Our poems are part of ourselves', he once wrote. Understanding the man helps us to better understand these poems, which can now be seen to have met pressing psychological needs, and emerge as fascinating aesthetic byproducts of the enthusiasms and anxieties, lusts and guilts, frustrations and aspirations of a vital human being.

Acknowledgments

Parts of this book have been adapted from articles that appeared in *The Cambridge Quarterly* and *English: The Journal of the English Association*. Extracts from John Betjeman's *Collected Poems* are reproduced by permission of Hodder and Stoughton.

Abbreviations

CP John Betjeman, *Collected Poems* (London: John Murray, 2006).

L1 *John Betjeman: Letters, vol. 1: 1926-1951*, ed. Candida Lycett Green (London: Methuen, 2006).

L2 *John Betjeman: Letters, vol. 2: 1952-1984*, ed. Candida Lycett Green (London: Methuen, 2006).

CH *John Betjeman, Coming Home: An Anthology of Prose*, selected and introduced by Candida Lycett Green (London: Methuen, 1997).

1

COMFORT POETRY?

The only constant, sitting there,
Patient and hairless, is a bear.

– CP, p350

'ARCHIBALD', JOHN BETJEMAN'S VERSE TRIBUTE TO his
lifelong companion, was published in 1982, the year in which
The Times appointed this knighted Laureate 'Teddy Bear to the
Nation'.[1] Evidently he was to be treasured, but not taken seriously.
Truth be told, it was as much Betjeman the broadcaster as
Betjeman the versifier who had found a soft spot in English hearts.
A regular presence on radio and television since the late 1950s,
he was one of few presenters from those pioneering days who
actually seemed to be enjoying himself in front of the camera.
The on-screen Betjeman is by turns genial, ingenuously enthused,

---

[1] Alan Bell, 'Sir John Betjeman – By Appointment: Teddy Bear to the Nation',
The Times (20 September 1982), p5.

distracted, occasionally nonplussed: a disarming act. And we shall see that the need to disarm – both his audience and aspects of his own life and character that caused him anxiety – lies near the root of Betjeman's art, which, I want to suggest, is less comforting than might at first be assumed. But there was enough in his stanzas that corresponded to the affably eccentric man on the telly for middle-brow British book-buyers to warm to this poet as they had to no other, and if there's one poem that encapsulates his winning formula it has to be 'A Subaltern's Love-song', with its celebrated game of tennis:

> Miss J. Hunter Dunn, Miss J. Hunter Dunn,
> Furnish'd and burnish'd by Aldershot sun,
> What strenuous singles we played after tea,
> We in the tournament – you against me!
>
> Love-thirty, love-forty, oh! weakness of joy,
> The speed of a swallow, the grace of a boy,
> With carefullest carelessness, gaily you won,
> I am weak from your loveliness, Joan Hunter Dunn.
>
> *– CP,* p87

It's hard to believe that the Blitz was raging when this doctor's daughter and her beau were introduced to the world – Aldershot, home of the British Army, would have been buzzing with military activity – but in John Betjeman's alternative reality all such disruptive influences are held effortlessly at bay. The dippy speaker welcomes us into a privileged space where everything is reassuringly as and where it should be: the tennis racket is in its press; the BBC news is on time (no matter what's on the news); a bracing aperitif is to hand. Even the horticulture, under benevolent paternal control, appears to be glowing with health ('Her father's euonymus shines as we walk'). Betjeman had a knack for hitting on the unexpected but unsubstitutable word, and Dr Hunter Dunn's shrub – a specimen as ubiquitous in large English gardens as it is euphonious in this context – is the only genus that will do here. Just as the singles could only ever have been 'strenuous'. Certainly there's not much sign of strain in these stanzas: if everything in the Betjeman garden is rosy, then everything in his prosody is regular. As those trademark dactyls waltz faultlessly through the quatrains, it all looks like pure escapism, comfort poetry for those who do not wish to be disturbed.

This feeling that John Betjeman was – like Archie his bear – a comforter, his verses fashioned to put the reader at ease and to set the mind at rest, marked him out as offering not only a welcome distraction from the war effort and subsequent post-war privation, but also an accessible alternative to the brain and form-bending discomforts of modernism. Where in 1921 the creator of another love song persona, the distinctly unteddyish T.S. Eliot, had asserted that 'poets in our civilization, as it exists at present, must be *difficult*',[2] Betjeman – a generation younger and very much a product of the frivolous 1920s – made it all look only too easy. As he put it in his 1960 verse autobiography 'Summoned by Bells', 'my urge was to encase in rhythm and in rhyme | The things I saw and felt (I could not *think*)' (*CP*, p408). That's partly light-hearted self-deprecation, partly heartfelt

---

[2] Eliot, 'The Metaphysical Poets', in *Selected Essays* (London: Faber and Faber, 1951), pp281-91, p289.

suspicion of the 'meddling intellect':[3] the poet indicated his Romantic affiliations by reviving the long-outmoded blank verse of Wordsworth and Tennyson for his own quixotic exploration of the (in this case) lack of growth of a poet's mind. In an age that prized innovation and complexity, such a combination of hackneyed form and ingenuous content constituted a statement of counter-cultural aesthetic allegiances that was, in its own way, as provocative as the one that Eliot had made nearly fifty years earlier. But if he was anachronistically closer to 19th-century modes of expression than modernist ones, then it's an indicator of Betjeman's originality that the tone of his poetry differs radically from both, not least in the way that – where Wordsworth, Tennyson and Eliot all compel their reader to take them seriously – Betjeman consistently invites us to take him lightly. J Alfred Prufrock might protest that he is not Prince Hamlet and wear the bottom of his trousers rolled, but the untranslated extract from Dante's *Inferno* that prefaces his love song gives us a pretty clear idea of the imaginative circles in which his creator moved. The author of 'Summoned by Bells' was himself not averse to a bit of name-dropping (including that of Eliot, by whom – in a bizarre coincidence – the schoolboy Betjeman was briefly taught), but he was more of a natural at playing the fool. When, presented with his pupil's self-published poems, the American Master remains tactfully silent, our reflecting poet chooses to savour the extraneous but nevertheless memorable fact that Eliot's judgement ('He thinks they're bad') was passed on by 'a boy called Jelly'.[4]

---

[3] Wordsworth, 'The Tables Turned', *William Wordsworth*, The Oxford Authors, ed. Stephen Gill (Oxford: Oxford University Press, 1984), p131.

He had these silly moments. Subsequently, critics were to less often reject Betjeman's poetry as simply bad than cheapen it as light, a word that's been used either as faint praise ('this excellent writer of light verse', as Janet Adam Smith put it) or more explicit censure (such as John Wain's assertion that Betjeman's tendency to write 'in metres usually associated with light and comic verse' reflected his 'almost complete lack of the skills of the true poet').[5] And yet, for all its simplicity and occasional silliness, those more sympathetic to his writing have found it strangely difficult to categorise. When, in 1962, Jocelyn Brooke asked if Betjeman should be classified as 'mere entertainer' or 'serious literary artist', he felt 'tempted to answer "yes" to both questions'. When, twenty years later, Patrick Taylor-Martin set out to redefine Betjeman as 'a serious, not to say profound, writer rather than the facile light versifier some people take him to be', he ended up describing him as 'predominantly a giver of pleasure: an entertainer, if you will'. And when, another quarter of a century on (the lengthy gaps between revaluative efforts tell their own story), Greg Morse once again asked the fundamental question 'so what exactly *is* Betjeman?' he came to the conclusion that this writer 'never quite fits in anywhere'.[6] John Betjeman is the definitive *sui generis* poet.

---

[4] (see opposite page) *CP*, p417. Betjeman elsewhere admitted that Eliot had reminded him of the incident: see Betjeman, 'The Usher of Highgate Junior School', in *T.S. Eliot Symposium* (Chicago: Regnery, 1949), pp89-92.

[5] Both quoted in Bevis Hillier, *John Betjeman: The Biography* (London: John Murray, 2006), p376, p392.

[6] Brooke, *Ronald Firbank and John Betjeman*, Writers and their Work series, (London: Longmans, Green for the British Council and the National Book League, 1962), p40; Taylor-Martin, *John Betjeman - His Life and Work* (London: Allen Lane, 1983), p7, p180; Morse, *John Betjeman: Reading the Victorians* (Eastbourne: Sussex Academic Press, 2008), p189, p190.

Pinning him down is like trying to nail jelly to the wall. His best readers have instinctively recognised that neither approval as substantial nor dismissal as lightweight quite hits the mark, and that to catch the Betjeman tone we need to find some way of accommodating both of these categories.

So that's the challenge for this book, and for an indication of my own jelly-nailing technique we could take a look at events that follow that game of tennis in Aldershot. 'A Subaltern's Love-song' moves with the light-footedness aspired to by those attending the 'dance at the Golf Club' so restlessly anticipated by its speaker, but it's not hard to recognise the effort that's gone into conjuring an impression of effortlessness here. This is 'carefullest carelessness' indeed, and the phrase speaks of more than just the craftsmanship for which W.H. Auden, somewhat condescendingly, admired his Oxford contemporary.[7] To offer another oxymoron, it reflects the calculated insouciance with which Betjeman approached his art, and indeed public life in general. If that makes him sound unappealingly disingenuous then it is important to go a stage further and discern the motives behind his method. I think it's safe to assume that John Betjeman – 'more Sybarite, for sure, than Stoic', to borrow a line from his biographer – would rarely have consulted Seneca, but the Roman philosopher's observation that 'nothing is burdensome if taken lightly' could be regarded as the unwritten instruction behind much of his poetry.[8] There's a difference between light verse and

---

[7] See Auden's introduction to *Slick but not Streamlined: Poems and Short Pieces by John Betjeman* (New York: Doubleday, 1947), pp9-16.

[8] Hillier, pxviii; Seneca, *Letters from a Stoic*, trans. Robin Campbell (Harmondsorth: Penguin, 2004), p226.

verse that deliberately makes light, as Betjeman does in his most famous poem when he gestures facetiously to the derangement ('how mad I am'), misery ('sad I am') and enervation ('oh! weakness of joy') of romantic infatuation. Those who make light of things have often felt something of their weight, a burden just hinted at when the Subaltern contemplates the tilt of Miss Hunter Dunn's nose, her harmonious tones, 'And the scent of her wrap, and the words never said, I And the ominous, ominous dancing ahead' (p88). 'Ominous': one of those trademark Betjeman dactyls. He pronounced it *ohminous*. It's a surprising word choice here, doubly so when repeated for emphasis. 'Ominous' shifts us, almost imperceptibly and just momentarily, from a world of reclaimed 1920s liberties to one of anticipated 1930s accountability; from the irresponsibility to be enjoyed in the shade of one's future father-in-law's euonymus, to the looming responsibilities that are perhaps just dawning on this husband-to-be. Because those never said words are going to have consequences: they herald engagement and commitment for a hitherto blithe speaker. Like the sun that settles questioningly on Joan's 'low-leaded window', this junior officer has question-popping in his thoughts. J Alfred Prufrock he isn't, but you do sense that the light verse is ending just as things are about to get heavy for him. And Betjeman knew exactly what he was going to go through, because it seems that – as well as the charms of Joan Hunter Dunn – he had his own courting days in mind when he wrote this poem. Unlike Joan, Penelope Chetwode, who Betjeman married in 1933, had spent much of her youth in Aldershot where, according to her granddaughter Imogen Lycett Green, her father 'manicured with an obsessive pride [...

] two grass tennis courts' which he considered 'second in perfection only to Wimbledon'.[9] Their marriage would turn out to be a quarrelsome one.

That one of this writer's most frivolous and buoyant poems should contain, near its conclusion, this fleeting indicator of gravity can be taken as indicative of the fact that consequential matters are not so much absent from Betjeman's work as lurking around its margins. The comforting, reassuring features scattered so liberally through 'A Subaltern's Love-song' themselves imply an unusually insistent need for comfort and reassurance. Scratch the glib surface and you often disclose an underlying anxiety in Betjeman, an impression that disturbing feelings and serious issues are being held at bay within the verse. The final lines of 'Summoned by Bells', for example, generate a similarly *ohminous* effect as 82 pages of predominantly sanguine and often frankly forgettable nostalgia are concluded by three lines that invite us to reconsider the whole exercise in light of significant new information: the author, afflicted by the vexations of age, chooses to belatedly inform us that he is now 'richer, wickeder and colder' (*CP*, p481). It's a phrase that sticks in the mind, functioning like a small black cloud passing over the sun on an otherwise clear day. Just as this self-confessedly degenerate old narrator casts a chilly shadow over the innocent joys of his own youth, so shadowy presences often lie concealed in the shrubbery of Betjeman's whimsically versified suburbia. Greg Morse puts it melodramatically, but his point stands: this poet's charming

---

[9] Imogen Lycett Green, *Grandmother's Footsteps: A Journey in Search of Penelope Betjeman* (Basingstoke: Macmillan, 1994), p3.

gardens are 'merely the calm surface to a maelstrom of deeper angst' (*Reading the Victorians*, p6).

The superficial gloss of Betjeman's poems makes it easy to overlook the burden of care, insecurity and frustrated desire that's often implied within them, and their author – bent on sustaining his disarming act (Anthony Powell, in a much-repeated bon mot, described Betjeman as having a 'whim of iron') – rarely drew attention to this burden directly. But the fact that there *is* often another dimension operating in this writing, and that the poet knew what he was about, is evidenced by the second of five precepts he once outlined in a letter to a protégé:

1) Poetry should not be private but easy for all to understand
2) It should have tones of meaning beyond the surface one
3) It should read out loud well
4) It should be memorable
5) It should very clearly not be prose. Rhythm helps make it different.

– L1, p472

Precept number two seems a little out of place here, but those concealed tones of meaning signal the potential for emotional (if not conceptual) complexity in Betjeman's ostensibly simple verses. And even if the other four principles reflect the aesthetic conservatism with which this writer was associated, the motivation behind his rhyme-and-scan approach to versifying can't be reduced to thoughtless traditionalism. Recrudescing in the mid-twentieth century, the pre-modernist register that Betjeman restored seemed at the time as anachronistic, and was as widely disparaged, as the Victorian architecture that he also famously championed. The arrival, via the American Master, of *vers libre* into English poetry had made the ornate regularity of traditional stanzas look patently inadequate as a means to apprehend the shifting influences of disruption to which the modern mind was sensitised. But Denis Brown is right to note that Betjeman's dependable rhythmic patterns often feel like a 'mode of containment [...] a comfort structure (a kind of verse teddy bear), even when the content is disturbing'.[10] John Donne, that 'difficult' poet who Eliot believed had 'first made it possible to think in lyric verse',[11] seems as unlikely an ally as Seneca for our simple poet who assures us that he 'could not *think*', but in his attempt to aesthetically corral the unruly emotions to which (as we shall see) he was deeply susceptible, Betjeman was following Donne's prescription in 'The Triple Fool':

> I thought, if I could draw my pains
>   Through rhyme's vexation, I should them allay.
> Grief brought to numbers cannot be so fierce,
> For he tames it, that fetters it in verse.[12]

No doubt, in this context, the Tennyson-loving poet would himself have recalled a stanza from 'In Memoriam':

> But, for the unquiet heart and brain,
> A use in measured language lies;

---

[10] Brown, *John Betjeman*, Writers and their Work series (Plymouth: Northcote House, 1999), p8.

[11] Eliot, 'Donne in our Time', in *A Garland for John Donne 1631-1931*, ed. Theodore Spencer, 2nd edn. (Gloucester Mass: Peter Smith, 1958), pp3-19, p16.

[12] Donne, *Complete English Poems*, ed. A.J. Smith (Harmondsworth: Penguin, 1976), p81.

The sad mechanic exercise,
Like dull narcotics, numbing pain.[13]

Happy mechanic exercises can also do the job. Where successive generations of his academically-sanctioned contemporaries – modernist, apocalyptic, confessional, myth-making – distorted verse forms in an effort to evoke states of anxiety, fear and desire, a contumacious John Betjeman, playing the fool who is 'a little wise' (as Donne puts it), sought to fetter similar forces within (for example) the foursquare rhythms of *Hymns Ancient and Modern*, the crowd-pleasing lilt of ballad metre, or the outmoded waltz of dactyls. Moments when this waltz threatens to slip into a minor key and turn into a *danse macabre*, as it does when the Subaltern contemplates the ominous, life-changing event he's about to attend, alert us to the presence of disruptive influences that the 'numbers' have been constraining.

Insecurity, loneliness, lust, fear. The tones of meaning hidden beneath the superficial whimsy of John Betjeman's poems are often surprisingly dark. One senses that, as much as his reader, it was the poet himself whose mind was to be set at rest and feelings put at ease by the comforts described in, and the comforting rhythms of, his verses. He was a man much drawn to sources of reassurance: the presence of the bear; the weekend in the country house; the rocking of the railway carriage; the consolation of strong but sympathetic women (both real and imaginary); the solace of alcohol and, later in life, tranquillisers ('He often told me he would like to be in a wheelchair taking valium every day', his daughter Candida recalled, *L2*, p372). The same neediness

---

[13] Tennyson, *Selected Poems* (Harmondsworth: Penguin, 1991), p134.

can be felt as a persistent ache deep in the bones of his poetry. In his introduction to the 2006 edition of the *Collected Poems*, fellow Laureate Andrew Motion noted Betjeman's repetition of the word 'safe', which 'appears like a nervous tic in his poems' (*CP*, pxx), and which the poet applies as an epithet to Archie the bear in 'Summoned by Bells' (*CP*, p400). According to this record of his formative years, the sense of vulnerability that was to haunt this man throughout his life was born early. The poem 'False Security' (*CP*, pp212-13), which recalls a childhood birthday party, catches it nicely. There is his involuntary reaching for the reassurance of comforting familiarities, evident here in snugly fitting attire and the characteristic naming of once-familiar high street shops of the kind frequented by nurturing middle-class mothers:

> Oh who can say how subtle and safe one feels
> Shod in one's children's sandals from Daniel Neal's,
> Clad in one's party clothes made of stuff from Heal's?

But the poem concludes with anxiety, a feeling of inadequacy, a fear of rejection, as overheard words puncture the child's pride at being the party's final leaver (an unidentified mother describes him, in jarring upper-case, as a 'STRANGE, RATHER COMMON LITTLE BOY'). The fact that, as he records in 'Narcissus' (*CP*, pp280-81), his father was 'in trade' was an enduring cause of discomfort for the young Betjeman, a dedicated social climber who counted future peers among his University peers, but his unease was not limited to feelings of embarrassment regarding the class into which he had been born. 'Summoned by Bells' reveals that he also felt guilt for not following his father into the family business; in 'Narcissus' it is his mother's incomprehensible admonitions regarding his nascent sexuality that leave this 'delicate' child, once again, clinging for security to his bear. Class shame was just one aspect of a more pervasive insecurity.

Betjeman's increasingly threadbare bear never seems to have been fully relieved of his initial duty to keep these many worries at bay. When, in one of those shadowy moments where the insecure adult intrudes on the narrative of 'Summoned by Bells', the poet recalls a 'dreadful day' when Archie was taken away as a form of punishment, he finds he is still moved to seek reassurance:

> Sometimes the desolation of that loss
> Comes back to me and I must go upstairs
> To see him in the sawdust, so to speak.
>
> – *CP*, p400

Such adult reversions to the infantile remind us that this poet was not averse to looking 'utterly ridiculous' (as a contemptuous Tom Paulin once described him),[14] but they also signal the presence of enduring anxieties. For ultimately neither teddy bear nor tidy verses could allay the fears. Indeed, the mere fact of his continuing presence in Betjeman's adult life seems to have made Archie – source of childhood companionship but also symptom of childhood insecurity – less ursine tranquilliser than nagging reminder of unresolved apprehension. Archie grew up to be the least cuddly of teddies, his imaginary life as a fire-and-brimstone non-conformist preacher being symptomatic of an uncompromisingly judgemental streak.[15] So when we look more

---

[14] 'New Views on Betjeman: The Teddy Bear and his Critics', *The Listener* (23 May 1985), pp20-21.

[15] Not to mention his flirtation with Nazism: 'it is Nuremberg manufacture that must have done it', Betjeman surmised. See *L1*, p263.

closely into the woollen eyes depicted in his eponymous poem we shouldn't be surprised to see something quite the opposite of comfort:

> He has no mouth, but seems to say:
> 'They'll burn you on the Judgement Day.'
>
> *— CP*, p349

It's a joke, of course, but one that's typical Betjeman in so far as the line which gets the laugh is also – given the author's sincerely held if distinctly challenged Christian faith – the one which should be taken most seriously. Wry humour to make light of dark forebodings. The poem 'Archibald', an ambiguous tribute if ever there was one, sees this supposedly 'safe' old bear transformed from confidante into inquisitor, from guarantor of sweet dreams to the stuffed stuff of nightmares, the mouthless voice of retribution that signals this poet's distressing sense of his own unatoned sinfulness and expectation of ultimate punishment.

Archie points his unerring paw towards the areas of sin and insecurity that I want to explore in this book. If Betjeman's verses seem both slight and substantial at the same time, then this is the heavy stuff that constituted the burdensome motivating force of his poetic imagination, the ballast in the gondola beneath the hot air balloon of his frivolity, if you like. The poet succinctly identified the major constituents of this freight in a 1966 interview when he listed, as his main themes, the facts that 'you're all alone, that you fall in love, that you've got to die' (quoted in Hillier, p438). In practice, these strands are interwoven through the fabric of his *Collected Poems*, but – for convenience's sake – we might look at them one at a time.

'You fall in love'

As far as the most superficially appealing of the three is concerned, Betjeman was unabashedly responsive to the charms of physical beauty, be it female, male, or somewhere in between. He evoked the sheer exhilaration of a romantic encounter with considerable élan:

> The waltz was played, the songs were sung,
>   The night resolved our fears;
> From bunchy boughs the lime trees hung
>   Their gold electroliers.

With its common metre and stock images – not only a waltz but a moon and even a red rose – 'In the Public Gardens' (*CP*, p234) is easy enough to discount as derivative light verse, but perhaps the mood is better caught if its quatrains are seen as determinedly low-gravity. The poem is so light that it floats: riding the airs of Strauss (light music, of course), the imagery rises effortlessly upwards, a sense of buoyancy generated by the vertical layering of radiant effects, from evocative period lighting exotically hung in redolent branches via floodlights and on to the lovers' moon. This is what it feels like to be swept off your feet. The elated couple may be xenophobically distinguished from their grosser company by nationality, but it's really the revelation of reciprocated love that refines them, marks them out as special, and that transforms an anonymous municipal park into a private, shimmering space: another of John Betjeman's charmed gardens.

This poem trips the light fantastic with precious little suggestion of *danse macabre,* and yet there are those undefined 'fears'... Why even mention them? Is it hinted that their resolution might be temporary, for one special night only? And what exactly does the speaker mean when – in lines that, characteristically, seem at once the most amusing and the most psychologically loaded – he describes the couple as 'You so white and frail and pale | And me so deeply me'? Is this an idealistic assertion of authentic feeling as the man falls head over heels, or an ironic admission that he is what he is: capriciously susceptible to such momentary enthusiasms and passing infatuations? The poem is, after all, less about perfectly reciprocated love than it is about an on/off relationship, pointedly noted in its own entry and exit stanzas: '*Ausgang* we were out of love | *Und eingang* we are in'. Biographical knowledge that the verses memorialise a special moment in his extra-marital relationship with Elizabeth Cavendish (who was most definitely *not* 'frail' – the description is a private joke) only adds to a nagging feeling that things may be less straightforward and resolved here than the clichéd romantic imagery suggests. Matters of substance, we sense, are being deftly skirted: John Betjeman's speciality.

Most characteristic are love poems that make no secret of the intensity, not to mention the transgressive nature, of their speaker's carnal urges, and yet at the same time defuse any disruptive potential through humour, through making light of lust. A late example is 'Lenten Thoughts of a High Anglican' (*CP,* pp310-11), with its materialistic appreciation of an unidentified 'Mistress':

How nonchalantly she wears her clothes,
   How expensive they are as well!
And the sound of her voice is as soft and deep
   As the Christ Church tenor bell.

The *Private Eye* parody of this poem is irresistible –

Lovely lady in the pew
Goodness, what a scorcher, phew!
What I wouldn't give to do
Unmentionable things to you!

– although the original, published in the poet's last volume, is already something of a self-parody: Betjeman, with his by-then-notorious penchants for well-heeled women and church bells here preposterously combined, is playing himself.[16] The sentiment – in Grosvenor Chapel, in Lent, and with the author having just been appointed Poet Laureate – is *so* inappropriate that it is impossible to take seriously: it's a disingenuous confession whereby transgressive desire is neutralised by self-evident playfulness. 'Old Betje' is just being a ludicrous lech again; no harm done, apparently, either to the 'Mistress' or to the poet himself. But we shall see that an element of harm (and indeed self-harm) can lie hidden in the superficial charm of this man's love poetry. The degree of playfulness is often directly proportionate to the potential seriousness of the underlying

---

[16] The poet, who had started writing for *Private Eye* during the previous year, imitated himself on more than one occasion: 'Indoor Games Near Newbury' started life as his own late entry into a *New Statesman* competition to write a poem 'in the Betjeman manner' (see William S. Peterson, *John Betjeman: A Bibliography*, Oxford: Clarendon Press, 2006, p426.)

concern, in this case the incompatibility between the poet's faith and his susceptibility to extramarital infatuations, trivialised as the parson admonishes those members of his congregation with wandering eyes in the last two stanzas, but in truth a persistent source of anguish for this lustful parishioner. As one of the aged Betjeman's closest female companions Margie Geddes observed, 'he was a highly sexed man, practically to his death'.[17]

John Betjeman's tendency to fall inappropriately in love was one to which his bear bore disapproving witness. In 'Archibald', the teddy's reminder that his owner is fifty years nearer Hell is immediately followed by authorial self-recrimination and a stab of sexual remorse over the pretty faces that he has kissed. The stresses and guilts associated with illicit desire – temporarily transcended in the elation of 'In the Public Gardens', circumvented by humour in 'Lenten Thoughts of a High Anglican' – elsewhere exert a subtle but profound gravitational pull that implicitly roots Betjeman's fantasised gratifications in a real world of disruptive longings and evaded responsibilities. His 'amatory' poems, as they're labelled in the subtitle of 1940 volume *Old Lights for New Chancels* (the poet preferred the more straightforward term 'sexy'), adopt a variety of approaches by which hedonistic fleshly pleasures might be evoked, but also by which the emotional pressures associated with frustrated (and sometimes consummated) desire might be released.

---

[17] Quoted by Andrew Geddes, 'To be with John Betjeman was to enter another world' (*The Spectator*, 20 January 2007), p18.

'You're all alone'

In 'The Ecstacy', Donne's meditation on the refining power of reciprocated romantic feeling, the poet celebrates love's capacity to remedy existential solitude:

> When love, with one another so
>   Interinanimates two souls,
> That abler soul, which thence doth flow,
>   Defects of loneliness controls.
>
> – *Complete English Poems*, p55

Betjeman's fantasy women, whether blatantly adored on the tennis court or surreptitiously worshipped in church, provide – for the space of a poem at least – the sort of compelling distraction that alleviated the burden of loneliness that he felt. No man is an island, and John Betjeman would appear to have been the *least* isolated of men; indeed, it's hard to envisage him on his own, without family, partner, secretary, friends, associates, audience, producer or camera crew. Or bear, of course. But this tells its own tale, as gregariousness often reflects a dissatisfaction with one's own company, a craving for external validation, or for what is perceived to be a missing intimacy. Archie – self-pityingly described by his owner in 1972 as 'the one tangible thing that doesn't let me down' (*L1*, p.5) – had once provided this reassuring company for John the only child. As he puts it in 'Archibald', whatever the situation he found himself in, the 'ugly unrepentant bear' was always around. In adulthood this man continued to look for a significant other with whom he could share his experiences, and if no suitable candidate was available an imaginary one could be conjured up in a poem. One of Betjeman's distinguishing characteristics as a writer lies in the way he could temporarily lose himself not only in a place but also a persona, in the experience of being someone somewhere somewhen. He was a talented mimic, and in some poems it's a case of mockery by means of a (not-always) funny voice: 'The Town Clerk's Views' (*CP*, pp144-47), 'The Costa Blanca' (*CP*, pp308-09), 'Executive' (*CP*, pp312-13) and 'Advertising Pays' (*CP*, pp353-54) fall into this category. But where there is some emotional investment in his occupation of the existential spaces inhabited by others, the poetry seems both more engaging and more effective as a remedy for existential isolation.

One such poem is 'Thoughts on *The Diary of a Nobody*' (*CP*, pp218-19), which follows the fictional Mr and Mrs Pooter as they pass the well-to-do residences of Victorian Muswell Hill on their way to dine with friends. In its dutiful description, the mannered politeness of its language, its diligently correct iambic tetrameter, its ingenuous rhymes and orderly quatrains, this poem exudes Pooterishness. Charles would undoubtedly have been most pleased to pen such worthy lines. Indeed, until a cynically comic ending, you almost forget that Betjeman is there at all:

> Dear Charles and Carrie, I am sure,
>   Despite that awkward Sunday dinner,
> Your lives were good and more secure
>   Than ours at cocktail time in Pinner.

But this of course is what makes the poem typical. Betjeman's 'me' is never 'so deeply me' as when he is being someone else, a skill that I think reflects his desire to imaginatively annex the living space of others and, by so doing, temporarily lose sight of his own self. Or at least the bad and vulnerable aspects of that self: notably, it's the 'good' and 'secure' nature of the Pooters' coupledom that attracts the speaker. The fact that the security of Betjeman's own marriage was, at time of writing, being sorely tested by doctrinal divergence, as Penelope converted to Roman Catholicism, constitutes a significant element of the hidden, underlying disturbance here. It's no coincidence that the dependability of the Pooter marriage is evoked through the period detail of 'morning prayer', a ritual that, at this stage, the Betjemans were no longer sharing. And Penelope would have got the message: one of many amusing moments in her correspondence with her husband reflects her own love for this particular episode of *The Diary of a Nobody*: 'He tells me Emily has LEFT poor Zimmer and gone off to Hawaii with a lover', she reports, 'and that his sister had left her husband. I felt rather like Mr Pooter as all his relatives I asked after had – not died – but left their hubbies'.[18]

Documentary producer Kenneth Savidge recalls that Betjeman 'was always sneaking off' when they were on location together: 'I remember losing him completely in the village of Eddington – *eventually* I found him an hour later in the pub with the drivers' (*L2*, p257). The *Collected Poems* is littered with the verse equivalents of sneaking off to the pub with the drivers, or to lunch with the Pooters. Just as the emphasis on safety in Betjeman's poetry is born out of fearful insecurity; just as the superficial frivolity of his love poems camouflages a genuine emotional susceptibility; so his empathetic ability to lose himself in other

---

[18] Undated letter, British Library Betjeman Archive, Add. 71652. For Charles Pooter's faux pas, see Grossmith, George and Grossmith, Weedon, *The Diary of a Nobody* (Ware: Wordsworth Classics, 1994), p139.

lives, other places, other times is I think symptomatic of an unrequitable yearning to escape the intrinsically isolated self. He was, as he puts it with Coleridgean emphasis in 'Before the Anaesthetic or A Real Fright', a 'man who smiled alone alone' (*CP*, p107).

'You've got to die'

'Before the Anaesthetic' is a poem about the fear of death, the other serious concern that verse both expressed and kept at bay for John Betjeman. Patrick Taylor-Martin, who identified this as 'the strongest emotion in his entire being', hears 'an authentically personal note' in the resulting poems of gloom, as they were classified in 1954's *A Few Late Crysanthemums* (*John Betjeman: His Life and Work,* p103, p106). Yet the man who made light of his own disreputable desires often performed a similar aesthetic sidestep with his discombobulating fears. 'One eye smiles, the other is gloomy', Betjeman once observed about his bear in a letter to Penelope (*L2*, p562), and the phrase could also be applied to the dual perspective operating in his poetry. In 'Archibald' the bear's owner observes that the woollen thread of his teddy's smiley gloomy eyes seems to say, 'In double-doom notes, like a knell: I "You're half a century nearer Hell"' (*CP*, p350), another punchline whereby the sentiment that a Christian ought by rights to take most seriously is communicated in such a way as to preclude seriousness. The underlying gloom of this poem is mitigated, in its final stanza, by the ridiculous spectacle of an old man suffering something close to a panic attack at the thought of an analyst depriving him of his teddy bear, but it's worth noting in this context that, according to his daughter, Penelope had once insisted that her husband 'see a psychoanalyst to rid him of what she termed his persecution mania' (*L1*, p198). When the consoling Christian vision of eternity set by God in the human heart cedes, in this poem, to draughty darkness, we sense that something genuinely unbearable might be hiding under the cover of facetiousness. Betjeman's exclamatory response ('oh my God') is both casual blasphemy and heartfelt appeal; by the end of 'Archibald', he seems to be half cuddling his old bear, half hanging onto him for dear life. In fact, for John Betjeman the deepest source of trepidation appears to have been less that he had to die, more that the grave would itself provide no relief, a vision of eternal damnation that – according to 'N.W.5 & N.6' (*CP*, pp231-32) – he had absorbed from his nurserymaid's horror at the thought of a vengeful God. 'I caught her terror then. I have it still', this poem concludes. That's not exactly comfort poetry.

Sometimes the forces of dissolution rear up and confront us with shocking directness in Betjeman's verse: there are some distinctly gruesome moments in the *Collected Poems*, although by confining these predominantly to the realms of mock-horror, the poet finds a way of both expressing and diminishing his fears – a variation on the sort of artistic coping mechanism that we often see him adopting when faced with aspects of existence that he found genuinely hard to negotiate. But for all his facetiousness, there was a side to this man that seems to have been compelled to look death straight in its grey, decaying face: his long track record as a visitor at Bart's Hospital in London, offering company and consolation to the sick and the dying, was only made public after his own passing. Perhaps empathising with the fears of others was a way for Betjeman to feel less isolated in his own: as we shall see, some of his most heartfelt poems evoke the emotional suffering that follows diagnosis, or is generally attendant on illness and old age. Certainly his rhetorical insouciance was generated in the face of a persistent awareness that things fall apart. As he put it in a late retrospective, 'Give me the bonus of laughter | As I lose hold' ('The Last Laugh', *CP*, p341).

*

'You're all alone, you fall in love, you've got to die'. It might come as a surprise to some that Britain's teddy bear bard dwelt obsessively on such matters, and that they are lurking in the neglected corners of poems that seem bent on charming us with their superficial conviviality. But there are photos of John Betjeman that reveal a distracted darkness in his gaze that contradicts the infectious laughter with which he was popularly associated. 'One eye smiles the other is gloomy'. Perhaps it's only when we recognise the proximity of these two features in his poetry that we start to grasp the nature of its intrinsic contrariness and uncomfortable emotional complexity, wherein – I would suggest – lies its true value. Nowhere do these qualities display themselves more beguilingly than in verses that relate the thrills, frustrations, compulsions and guilts associated with lust.

2

NOT ENOUGH SEX

THERE'S A WELL-KNOWN EXCHANGE IN the final episode of Jonathan Stedall's retrospective documentary series on Betjeman where the elderly poet – he had little over a year left to live – is asked if he has any regrets.[1] His celebrated reply (see chapter heading) was a characteristic one: the overly earnest, searching question always tended to elicit a mischievous, uncomplicated answer from this man. It's also a poignant moment, as the brevity which lies at the soul of the witticism was symptomatic of a genuine struggle to speak, due to the cumulative damage wrought by Parkinson's Disease and a series of strokes. Thirdly, most significantly for our understanding of his poetry, the answer is wholly consistent with a familiar strategy in Betjeman's verse, whereby we suspect that the phrase clearly not meant to be taken straight might also be the moment of absolute sincerity. No subject was more amenable to this aesthetic

---

[1] *Time with Betjeman*, BBC, 1982-3.

manoeuvre than sex. Nothing else generated such elation, nor such guilt. There's no doubt that, in Betjeman's love poetry, the sense of fun draws more attention to itself than the sense of sin, or the emotional complications that tend to accompany physical desires and relationships. But such complications are almost invariably implicit, functioning like a cloudy background wash in a watercolour, the significance – or even the existence – of which is easily overlooked because the colourful activity going on in the foreground is so diverting. Such is the case, as we have seen, in poems like 'A Subaltern's Love-song', 'In the Public Gardens' and 'Lenten Thoughts of a High Anglican'. Just occasionally, as we shall see, the fun goes missing altogether, leaving an unnervingly stark canvas staring us in the face.

Betjeman addresses the problem of lust most directly, and most tongue-in-cheek, in the early poem 'Senex' (*CP*, p76-77). 'Oh would I could subdue the flesh | Which sadly troubles me!' the speaker begins, in a mock-penitential tone accentuated by melodramatic exclamation. The poem's ironic title is a term that Carl Jung uses to describe the archetypal wise old man, wisdom here being associated with the ascetic subjugation of concupiscent urges. But Betjeman, who was hardly old when he wrote this, adopts instead the persona of a sexually-tormented Puritan, cruising the streets on his ludicrous tricycle, titillated by his proximity to the mere possibility of illicit activity, as implied (in his inflamed imagination) by bikes leaning on a hedge. This seedy man petitions God to whip away the dogs of lust, here 'not ferocious hounds but rather spaniels', as Patrick Taylor-Martin points out before he concludes that the speaker of this poem's 'interest in girls is as harmless and playful as the spaniels themselves', and that 'Betjeman's pleas for deliverance from the sins of the flesh' are therefore 'not to be taken too seriously' (*John Betjeman: His Life and Work*, p101). All of which is true, of course – it's hard to take an image of spaniels with 'buttocks' in their 'paws' too seriously. But neither can you discount the possibility that these spaniels may be hounds in disguise, and that, by belittling them, a hounded poet is holding them at bay. As Thoreau once wrote, 'when a dog runs at you, whistle for him'.[2] Where religion conspicuously fails here (kneeling to pray only brings 'bare knees' and 'sulky lips' to mind), poetry apparently succeeds: unruly appetites have been fettered in comic verse. In its insouciance, 'Senex' displays the kind of sexual continence that it begs for, becoming the remedy for its own sickness. It constitutes a nice example of what Taylor-Martin himself perceptively identified as the 'complex double bluff' at the heart of Betjeman's work: 'saying something which one feels sincerely in such a way that it appears insincere or, at least, mildly facetious, and relishing the apparent perversity' (*John Betjeman: His Life and Work*, p79). Poetry serves both as a conduit for libidinous energies, and – through humour – as a way of dissipating them.

Such energies could also be temporarily discharged by an imagined conquest, although Betjeman's besotted speakers are more often conquered than conquerors – hence effectively absolved of responsibility for their transgressions. The bushes burdened with fragrant bloom in 'The Licorice Fields at Pontefract' (*CP*, p155) bear witness to an ardent encounter

---

[2] *The Writings of Henry David Thoreau*, Volume VII, Journal I, 1837-1846, ed. Bradford Torrey (Boston: Houghton Mifflin and Company, 1906), p153.

between one of these passive narrators and a north-country siren:

> Red hair she had and golden skin,
> Her sulky lips were shaped for sin,
> Her sturdy legs were flannel-slack'd,
> The strongest legs in Pontefract.

Meet the Betjeman dominatrix: sulky lips (again); sturdy legs; a woman who wears the trousers.[3] Such features leave our speaker wilted and weakened by the passionate feelings that consume him, and readily adopting a submissive role as he imagines himself the captivated vassal of this strapping Yorkshire lass. As he does in 'Myfanwy', a poem about an equally authoritative 'ringleader, tom-boy, and chum to the weak' (*CP*, p70), there is a sense that – as well as seeking to disarm both his reader and the object of his affection with comedy – Betjeman is deliberately neutering his own narrator here through infantilisation. The concluding couplet of 'The Licorice Fields of Pontefract', in which the speaker envisages himself held in strong brown arms and bound by the coils of his beloved's flowing locks, recalls Yeats's 'Brown Penny', with its memorably mellifluous line 'I am looped in the loops of her hair'.[4] Both poets emphasise the inexperience of the male lover; both, in their own ways and for their own reasons, have their speaker adopting a sexually unthreatening, emasculated posture. But where Yeats is evidently playing it straight and appears to be out for sympathy, the submissive attitude of

---

[3] 'All my girls can always be interpreted as big strong boys', Betjeman wrote to William Plomer (*L1*, p446).

[4] *Collected Poems of W.B. Yeats* (London: Macmillan, 1934), p109.

Betjeman's speaker is at one and the same time more whimsical and more calculated. Perhaps he recognises that, where seduction is concerned, desire tempered by humour is likely to be less off-putting than desire tainted by self-pity?

Betjeman's babes may be formulaic caricatures, but they were almost invariably based on flesh and blood. Joan Hunter Dunn was indeed the tanned and sporty 'shock-headed' daughter of a GP: the poet admitted to a friend 'I wrote the verses in the character of a subaltern in Aldershot, but they were really my own imaginings about her' (L2, p291). The 'lovely lady in the pew' was model and fashion editor Joan Constantinidi; in a characteristically disarming move, Betjeman sent the poem she had inspired to her husband. To an admirer who enquired about the origins of two of his Irish love poems, he confessed 'I did meet a lady on a wet day in Dungarven when she was staying in Helvick and I was in Dublin [...] The name Moira McCavendish was as fortuitous as Greta Hellstrom. They are there for their euphony and for their faces and figures in the memory of, Yours sincerely, John Betjeman'.[5] And Pontefract's 'robber chief' was modelled on Pearl Wilkinson, who – with her sister Florrie – helped the Betjemans with domestic chores after the family moved to Farnborough in the autumn of 1945. According to the poet's daughter Candida Lycett Green, Pearl the farm-girl was 'red-haired', 'sunburnt', and her father was 'stunned' by her 'beauty' (L1, p367). She is named in the poem 'Agricultural Caress' ('Keep

---

[5] L2, p485. The poems are 'The Irish Unionist's Farewell to Greta Hellstrom in 1922' (inspired by Emily Hemphill, CP, pp118-19) and 'A Lament for Moira McCavendish' (a rather transparent mask for Elizabeth Cavendish, CP, pp249-50).

me from Thelma's sister Pearl! I She puts my senses in a whirl',
CP, p279), which was not to find its way into print until 1966 but
also appears to date from the Farnborough years; presumably
Betjeman held it back until his family had left the village, as Pearl
had married a near-neighbour in 1948.[6] The poet may have
tactfully delayed the publication of potentially compromising
verses like this, or relocated the action to distant and unlikely
settings such as Pontefract, or transmogrified his muses and made
light of his crushes in order to avoid causing scandal, but this
only contributes to an impression that the poetry may have been
holding some genuinely disruptive appetites at arm's length.

It's harder to pin down the original Pam, 'great big
mountainous sports girl' of 'Pot Pourri from a Surrey Garden'
(*CP*, pp45-6), but this frolicsome love poem looks like another
artistic by-product of frustrated lust and domestic discontent.
Betjeman purloined his title from an eminently respectable
Victorian gardener's diary, but noted in a 1958 radio broadcast
that 'this is a different kind of pot-pourri'.[7] The literal translation
of the quaintly fragrant term ('rotten pot' – originally it described
mixed meats served in a stew) provides a suitably corrupt base-
note for what turns out to be a surprisingly spicy poetic perfume.
Written when both wife Penelope and muse Myfanwy (Piper)
were nursing their first-born,[8] 'Pot Pourri from a Surrey Garden'
could be seen as a clandestine attempt to reclaim some female

---

[6] See Candida Lycett Green, *The Dangerous Edge of Things: A Village
Childhood* (London: Doubleday, 2005), p26.

[7] Quoted in Peterson, *John Betjeman: A Bibliography*, p449.

[8] Paul Betjeman was born in November 1937, Edward Piper December
1936, and the poem written in 1938.

attention from usurping infants. From the start it juxtaposes
dutiful parenting with a liberated youthful fleshly presence: 'Miles
of pram in the wind and Pam in the gorse track'. Given that
Betjeman self-confessedly disliked babies, I take the first half of
this line to be a negative description of necessary perambulation,
accompanied in this stanza by the sound of horses, animals that
the poet also frankly disliked (he felt that his horse-loving wife
devoted more attention to them than she did to him). The second
half of the line sees nubile Pam counterpointing mobile pram.
From her first appearance in the gorse track, she is associated
with suggestive passageways. Having trespassed over her
'boundary' into the private space of her garden, the speaker goes
on to reject the path by the pram before taking the 'beautiful' if
'slippery' alley that leads to Pam's 'bountiful body'. All of which
begs to be read as a (surprisingly indecorous) symbolic mapping,
and indeed penetration, of some intimate anatomy. The narrator
of 'Pot Pourri from a Surrey Garden', then, shuns both parental
responsibilities and mother / child intimacy for the fantasy of
sexually claiming a somewhat masculine sister / daughter. The
poem concludes in yet another suspiciously corporeal corridor
when its just-married couple are envisioned in church walking
together 'up the Butterfield aisle' – a Victorian ecclesiastical
architect the butt of a crude joke here, perhaps?[9] As Pam and
poet finally displace pram and ponies, the apparently facile
happily-ever-after ending to this poem could be read rather as a
thunderous, somewhat manic defiance of those upstanding

---

[9] William Butterfield is also namechecked in 'Myfanwy at Oxford' (*CP*,
pp71-2). As Greg Morse puts it, lifelong bachelor Butterfield was 'to sex
what Carlisle United is to the Premiership' (*Reading the Victorians*, p50).

members of the Surrey community who might come between the speaker and his wish-fulfilling 'bride'. Poetry gives Betjeman license for the kind of illicit 'embracement' that, at this point, was denied to him in life.

Hidden agendas abound in John Betjeman's diverting verses. The facetious double bluff was only one of several manoeuvres that he employed in his aesthetic negotiation of fleshly appetites; another strategy appears to have been the projection of one's own unconscious, unwanted or unacceptable urges onto others. So when the poet famously asks the 'friendly bombs' to 'fall on Slough' (*CP*, p20), the ostensible target of the satire – modern residential development – may actually just be collateral damage, as he specifically wants to take out the sexually rapacious and irritatingly *successful* double-chinned man (with his phallic hardwood desk) who tells rude jokes and 'washes his repulsive skin | In women's tears'. Similarly, 'The City' (*CP*, p7) is populated by fat-bottomed businessmen who have 'awkward hips', tell 'dirty jokes' (again), and yet also lay physical claim to the local girls, lending some colour to their lives and engendering some suspicions in their wives. These are early poems, written a long time before Betjeman – himself never averse to a dirty joke – developed his own awkward hips and large behind. Sometimes the anticipatory nature of the projection can be almost uncanny, as in the sequence of five poems – published before his wartime move to Ireland, before his extra-marital relationship, and 29 years before his knighthood – that recount the sexual misadventures of Sir John, the Irish 'Baronet Piers' (*CP*, pp59-68). Both men are the kind who like to be the life and soul, and, going by his own love poem, the fictional Sir John also shares the future Sir John's fondness for Gothic revival architecture and facial pigmentation: the Baronet Piers, his abbey soaring around him, professes to be drowning in love for his *acushla* with a freckled frown ('The Attempt', pp63-4). Betjeman wrote this sequence several years before he met his secretary Jill Menzies, who he adored and would rechristen 'Freckly Jill'. Like the sexual predators of 'Slough' and 'The City', it seems that the law of psychological projection demands that the naughty Baronet must be punished, and just deserts are meted out when his aforementioned *acushla* leaves him for abbeys new. Patrick Taylor-Martin's words on another Irish pastiche, 'A Lament for Moira McCavendish' (*CP*, pp249-50), could equally be applied to 'The Attempt': 'If this were no more than a tongue-in-cheek exercise in technique we would not be so moved. The very passion which underlies the poem lifts it above parody' (*John Betjeman: His Life and Work*, p145). I'm not sure we're exactly 'moved', but for all they may be pastiches, there is, nevertheless, evidently sincere feeling in both of Betjeman's Irish laments. The suffering of unfulfilled desire is integral to this feeling.

Elsewhere, rather than punishing them, the poet exempts sexual transgressors from blame – less projection than self-exoneration by proxy, perhaps? Oscar Wilde emerges from the Cadogan Hotel with considerably more style than the music hall policemen who come to arrest him (*CP*, pp16-17); the 'thumping crook' in a Bath teashop may be caught in the act of deception, but the moment is described as one when both seducer and seduced seem almost angelic, beatified (*CP*, p105); the euphemistically-indicated and probably-illicit relations of a couple now laid to rest in Willesden Churchyard (*CP*, p266-67), corresponding to the

probably illicit relations of the couple that pass their grave, are a
source of mildly salacious curiosity rather than censure:

> And this, my love, is Laura Seymour's grave –
> 'So long the loyal counsellor and friend'
> Of that Charles Reade whose coffin lies with hers.
> Was she his mistress?

More disturbingly, Rex, speaker of the dramatic monologue
'Shattered Image' (*CP*, pp326-31), is given significant space to
plead for our sympathy, and he uses it to shift the focus of attention
and moral censure onto the friends and associates who extricate
themselves from his society following the accusation of
paedophilia.

Then there are one or two poems about physical desire where
psychological diversion strategies appear to give way to a more
immediate and candid response, although even a half-comic, half-
confessional piece like 'Late-Flowering Lust' (*CP*, pp171-72) may
conceal a surprisingly complicated emotional situation. Beginning
with an unflattering self-portrait that identifies the speaker as a
jaded debauchee, this poem describes what at first appears to be
a clandestine rendezvous between two aging lovers (the 'brandy'
mentioned in stanza two being the kind of disinhibitor that might
be associated with such encounters). Yet the imagery that
accompanies their assignation is anything but lascivious.
Envisaging the couple's embrace as a skeletal clinch, the speaker
indulges in some characteristically ghoulish humour:

> Dark sockets look on emptiness
> Which once was loving-eyed,

>   The mouth that opens for a kiss
>   Has got no tongue inside.

As it turns out, this confession is characterised less by guilt than fear, as sex is associated with encroaching mortality rather than compromised morality. The embrace is one of needy mutual support rather than excited mutual exploration: 'I cling to you inflamed with fear | As now you cling to me'. In fact, the unexpected tone of this poem makes more sense if we see this 'reunion' as being not with a mistress, but with a recently and temporarily estranged spouse. 'Late-Flowering Lust' emerged from a uniquely turbulent phase in the Betjemans' marriage, with Anglican John struggling to come to terms with what he saw as Penelope's 'desertion' of their shared pew after she was received into the Church of Rome in March 1948.[10] The poem appears to have been written at some point during the following month, after an unusually long period of separation between the two (Penelope had spent time in Oxford, John in Cornwall and then Denmark). 'Reunion' is, perhaps, its key word. It suggests that this is no casual liaison or one-night stand, and if it is still possible that the encounter is being enjoyed with an old flame, other moments hint at the kind of long-term emotional bond more characteristic of a marriage than an affair: in stanza five, for example, the lines 'I feel how frail you are my dear | And wonder what will be' sound both genuinely solicitous and (in the term of address) distinctly conjugal. The word 'reunion' may also hold a suggestion of bitterness: John feared that Penelope's conversion had called their own union into question; he was affronted that,

---

[10] See 'The Empty Pew' (*CP*, p395).

'in the eyes of the Pope' at least, his wife was no longer married to him (*L1*, p440). The couple's shared concern regarding their matrimonial status remained serious enough for Penelope to seek ecclesiastical recognition of the marriage from the Vatican during May of 1949. The following year Betjeman acknowledged in a letter to his wife that he had been 'jealous of Rome [...] for further pulling us apart', and pleaded – in a sincere and serious tone that is unusual in their correspondence – for more periods of intimate contact ('seeing you and being with you alone much more than I am') so that they 'might grow more united' (*L1*, p460, p461). This, I think, is the context in which we should understand the shared trepidation, the panicky sense of insecurity about the future, that is so unexpectedly entwined with sensuality and humour in 'Late-Flowering Lust'. The couple's mutual clinging may in part be a reaction to the centrifugal force that had been generated by altered affiliations: 'Religious difference kills family affection, that is the tragedy of this event at present,' as Betjeman wrote to a friend in 1947 (*L1*, p422). The pair evidently remained united by an emotional and physical circuitry established over time; indeed, the poem suggests that their awareness of this connection had been heightened by separation, reactivated perhaps by the sense of a more consequential impending disunity; but the emphasis on physicality here – not only that of desire but also, significantly, that of decay – also reflects the loss of a reassuring common spiritual refuge.

John Betjeman faced an interesting challenge as a love poet. On the one hand, he was clearly driven to give some artistic expression to his experience of fleshly craving, not only to memorialise but also perhaps to sublimate these feelings; on the other, he was understandably wary about revealing the precise circumstances behind manifestations of these cravings, and about giving an impression of their urgency, the degree to which they really did possess and distress him. To adapt terms provided by 'Narcissus', the aesthetic challenge was to explore the 'most secret places' but also to 'leave no traces' (*CP*, p281). The struggle to square this circle can be discerned in the successive stanzas of 'A Russell Flint' (*CP*, p277), a piece that, in a succinct example of the embarrassment and contempt that Betjeman's love poetry can engender in some readers, A.N. Wilson has dismissed as 'one of his worst gush-poems'.[11] First 'leave no traces': the title here deliberately points to art rather than life, conveying something of its subject's beauty while depersonalising her in an attempt to camouflage both identifying features and the poet's emotional investment. Yet the person that really mattered – Betjeman's freckled secretary Jill – was fully aware who this was about:

> One evening, just before I left, he took me and his friend Christopher Hollis to the Garrick Club. I had never been anywhere like that before and was very excited. I went upstairs to the ladies' cloakroom to leave my coat; the excitement must have shown as I came downstairs.
>
> – *L2*, p14

This mutually breathtaking moment is caught in the poem's first two lines: 'I could not speak for amazement at your beauty | As you came down the Garrick stair'. By the end of this stanza the real woman is already being transformed into a generic Betjeman-type: the strict-but-kind floppy-haired senior schoolgirl

---

[11] Wilson, *Betjeman* (London: Arrow Books, 2007), p183.

muse. Such caricaturing both disguises the original and releases some of the emotional pressure caused by a stirring recollection: the poet is making light again. Yet when that first line is repeated, word for word, at the beginning of stanza four, we are reminded that the heart of this poem lies in one of those 'moments of ecstasy or depression' that Betjeman elsewhere identified as the true source of his creative urge (*L2*, p256). The 'depression' that accompanies unrequited love surfaces explicitly in the last stanza, as, drowning in the oceanic eyes of his muse (and beginning to sound a lot like the Baronet Sir John Piers), the speaker offers a frank expression of the emotional neediness that so often seems implicit in Betjeman's poetry: 'Hold me when the tide goes down', he plaintively concludes.

'Love makes us restless and we resist it', Betjeman wrote to playwright John Osborne following the first night performance of *Inadmissible Evidence* in 1964. On that evening he had seen his own dark side writ large in the play's unfaithful, misanthropic and self-loathing 'hero' Bill Maitland (*L2*, p384). Like many before him and since, John Betjeman's capacity to resist 'love' was, to say the least, limited, but ultimately not even this man could go on making light of such matters. If 'A Russell Flint' offers a rare glimpse of yearning offered relatively straight, then the need to confess amatory derelictions in a more direct fashion was to find its most explicit expression in a tale of remorse on a railway, 'Guilt' (*CP*, p365), a significant poem that was withheld from Betjeman's *Collected* and remained unpublished until two years before his death. Here the sense of despair so often concealed by this poet's frivolity is finally given stark expression:

I haven't hope. I haven't faith.
  I live two lives and sometimes three.
The lives I live make life a death
  For those who have to live with me.

The full significance of the passing gesture in the second line of this stanza only became apparent after Betjeman's death, when Andrew Geddes revealed the identity of a third woman in an article about his recently deceased mother's four-year affair with the poet. In itself, the revelation was hardly surprising: neither wife, nor 'another wife' (as the poet puts it in the similarly confessional 'Pershore Station', *CP*, p224), nor indeed another mistress could remedy what appears to have been a compulsive need. Such relationships were symptoms rather than cures. But the fact that, however fleetingly, Betjeman made this most compromising admission in a poem reflects the pressure that his conscience was exerting on him late in life. It reinforces our sense that, for this man, the means of light verse were employed to weighty psychological ends, albeit usually taking imaginatively circuitous routes towards these ends. At base Betjeman self-identified as a poet, so the inconvenient truth had to be told in a poem.

'Colonel' Kolkhorst, a mentor since his university days, had recognised in 1951 the potential damage that Betjeman's lifelong susceptibility to romantic infatuation might cause:

> Is it not about time you gave your heart a rest, for a little while anyway? You have been at it non stop now for I don't know how many donkey's years, it is not good for you [...] do get a rest and give your poor heart a holiday. It's become a sort of drug, love, and you've become a love fiend.
>
> – *L2*, p9

The charm concealed self-harm. But the love drug was also a high-octane fuel that drove the engine of Betjeman's poetry, hence the ambivalence noted by priest and confidant Harry Jarvis when he reflected on the subject of his friend's conscience: 'Sometimes I think that he thoroughly enjoyed dealing with guilt, to some extent anyway. He was happy some of the time but he went through long periods of being very, very unhappy and consumed with guilt' (*L2*, p154). More jelly-nailing. This potent and unstable mix, the energized emotional and creative agitation combined with a sense of sin, manifests as physical restlessness in 'Guilt', the end of which leaves us uncertain if our Christian sybarite is heading for ascetic renunciation or further indulgence. He follows an ill-defined urge to 'make retreat' that leads him, from the London streets,

> Into a warm electric train
>   Which travels sorry Surrey through
> Where, crystal-hung, the clumps of pine
> Stand deadly still beside the line.

This is a revealing, minor key counterpoint to earlier verses. The woods and railway lines of Surrey had once provided Betjeman with the backdrop for a tale of carefree trysting: the speaker of the early amatory poem 'Love in a Valley' (*CP*, p23) feels light-headed with self-abandonment as, amidst pine-trees and fragrant precipitation, she asks her Lieutenant to take her to his Surrey home. But even here a hint of the canvas was already peeking through, for the lover is also aware of the different kind of abandonment that awaits when her soldier is posted to China: the bright light of 'Love in a Valley' modulates from the flare of reckless and joyful passion to the painful glare that a 'brilliant arcade' casts on one subsequently reduced to a solitary window-shopping. Many years later, the icy glitter of 'Guilt' no longer illuminates the still-hopeful, straightforward romantic distress of youth and innocence, but rather the hopeless, contradictory, self-aware compulsions – both for indulgence and absolution – that accompany age and experience. Light in this poem has become an *ignis fatuus* that draws a speaker whose neurosis is signalled by ominous repetition: 'For somewhere, somewhere burns a light I To lead me out into the night.' Here is a man who knows that he is not in control of himself. At times like this Betjeman's poetry seems to be marking out territory wherein topographical detail is infused by the needs and distress generated by a sense of existential loneliness. It's territory that warrants further exploration.

3

ESCAPADES

'SORRY SURREY' ISN'T THE ONLY ENGLISH county named in John Betjeman's poetic corpus. The 'index of places' that was appended to the 2006 edition of his *Collected Poems* can be taken as an indicator of the importance that this writer attached to location. Betjeman, as his daughter noted, 'never tired of discovering new places'.[1] If sheer quantity is anything to go by, topography puts lust into the shade as the main wellspring of this man's poetic inspiration. The insistent place naming in his poem titles – I count 102 of the 233 in this book – could be regarded as a simple by-product of its author's desire to preserve in verse the things that he perceived and felt; it would be easy to assume that, just as he fought to save unfashionable buildings, so Betjeman identified obscure locations in a straightforward effort to preserve evanescent memories, as if he were labelling snapshots in a

---

[1] *Betjeman's Britain,* ed. Candida Lycett Green (London: Folio Society, 1999), p9.

photograph album. Yet you often sense that these place names are not only mnemonics but also verbal icons – they have a magic all of their own – and that what this poet does to place is as much transformative as it is preservative. In other words, location is not simply identified, but spotlighted and sanctified by the attention that's devoted to it. Betjeman not only described the places that he visited, he sprinkled them with the fairy dust of his creative imagination. He was, to borrow a phrase from Wallace Stevens' poem 'Description without Place', one of those 'for whom the word is the making of the world'.[2]

Sophisticated Stevens may seem as unlikely an ally for teddy bear Betjeman as difficult Donne or stoical Seneca, yet it's worth remembering that, if these two poets were to follow radically divergent branch lines, they shared a point of departure in aestheticism. The relish of language in Betjeman's topographical poetry reminds us of the intrinsic pleasure that he took in creative journeys, with reality only the station platform from which he departed. In fact, this arch-describer of place might usefully be read with other lines from Stevens' 'Description without Place' held in mind:

> Description is revelation. It is not
> The thing described, nor false facsimile.
>
> It is an artificial thing that exists,
> In its own seeming, plainly visible,

---

[2] *The Collected Poems of Wallace Stevens* (New York: Alfred Knopf, 1957), pp339-46, p345.

Yet not too closely the double of our lives,
Intenser than any actual life could be.

– Collected Poems, p344

An instinctive artificer, Betjeman transformed what he saw into a virtual reality more intense than the actual life that surrounded him. Take, for example, the vision of a 'grassy kingdom sweet to view' offered at the start of 'Church of England thoughts occasioned by hearing the bells of Magdalen Tower from the Botanic Garden, Oxford on St Mary Magdalen's Day' (*CP*, pp156-57), a ponderous title for some graceful stanzas. Focusing on 'Church of England thoughts' led Denis Brown to characterise this poem as an '*exemplum* of the Anglican middle way' (*John Betjeman*, p58), but – tonally – its spellbound evocation of Oxford's Botanic Garden is more indicative of the aesthete's magical way. The summons of his old college bells has clearly revived the undergraduate euphuist in Betjeman, who responds in this poem with his own tolling, Tennysonian tetrameter, patterns of assonance and alliteration embellishing the ornate diction ('umbelliferae', 'Linnaean symmetry', 'resin-scented chines', 'rhododendrons' and 'reredoses'). With 'tiger lilies' adding a touch of fin-de-siècle chinoiserie, this poem looks very much like the kind of fragile and exotic specimen that would be at home in a late-Victorian glasshouse. The garden's outsized wall contributes to our sense that we have entered a privileged microclimate here, although Betjeman is careful to avoid completely sealing off his other-world from the surrounding environment: when it anticipates traffic noise from the town, the final stanza breaks the aesthete's spell, keeping us at least in hearing distance of mundane reality. Betjeman's elysiums are invariably threatened like this, whether by the ugly workaday world, or by unsympathetic forces, or just by the passing of time. I would suggest that this insistent urge to sanctify place has its roots in the poet's psychological constitution. In this case, the main context is provided by his brief and inglorious academic career ('Failed in Divinity!', as – relishing the irony – he disbelievingly exclaims in 'Summoned by Bells', *CP*, p475). The resurgent aestheticism here is implicitly a rejoinder to those insensitive Oxford dons (most notoriously C.S. Lewis) who had been unable to recognise this young man's idiosyncratic qualities when he was a student at the University. Betjeman, having now made a name for himself beyond the college walls, is back to reconceive, and stake his own claim to, the little patch of Eden from which he was so callously ejected by those who he felt lacked the sensibility to truly appreciate it. Another personal context, this time for the celebration of 'moderate' worship and 'multiplicity' in this poem, is provided by his wife Penelope's conversion to the Church of Rome a few years earlier. More than one clandestine battle is being waged in this picturesque garden, then. As is often the case in Betjeman, a glossy veneer conceals matters of substance.

It may be significant that, where Betjeman was constantly straying into other people's houses and gardens, his own are all but missing from his poetry.[3] Some artists specialise in evoking their familiar locale; this one specialised in getting away (a phrase that would perhaps have been more suitable than *Coming Home*

---

[3] Two possible exceptions being 'Wantage Bells' (*CP*, p208) and 'On Leaving Wantage 1972' (*CP*, p296), although in neither case is it clear that the poet is describing his own domain.

as the title for an anthology of his prose). 'Winter at Home', a 1940s article reprinted in this book, paradoxically concludes with the poet indulging what he describes as 'the greatest winter joy' he knew: 'I shall take the train to the coast and spend a night by the sea' (*CH*, p157). Equally odd is the failure to mention his family in this essay about 'home'. No doubt the desire for privacy was a factor here, but Betjeman never really associated poetic creativity with his own domestic arrangements. I think the intense pleasure that he derived from visiting other places can only be understood in the context of an implied need to – temporarily, but regularly – leave old ones, and the responsibilities with which they were associated, behind. Traversing and describing hitherto uncharted regions offers one way to avoid having to dwell too exclusively on, and indeed in, realities with which we are only too well acquainted, and both John and Penelope were susceptible to wanderlust. Given his interest in exploring and imaginatively occupying the psychological as well as physical spaces of others, it may be the case that by travelling Betjeman was also seeking to be transported from overly familiar aspects of his own self: not his enthused and entertaining persona, who was invariably centre of attention and usually came along for the ride, but the man he had to come home to: morally flawed and easily bored, sometimes angry, anxious and frightened, troubled by frustrated desires and guilts, attended by family and friends yet still burdened by the nagging feeling that he was 'all alone'.

To catch the mood of Betjeman's topographical poems, then, we need to appreciate not only how they crystallise the spirit of a place, but also what they reveal about the spirits of a person. Three characteristic aspects help to disclose some of the more fundamental motivating forces behind verses that might at first seem merely descriptive or decorative. Firstly, there is the relish this man took not so much in destination as in anticipation: the intrinsic pleasure of the journey (both literal and creative); secondly, there is the emphasis that he places on intimacy and shared experience, as reflected in the roles that other people play in these on-location poems; third is this poet's capacity to become absorbed in the fine detail of his observations, which can be seen as a means of temporarily escaping the isolated self, as troubled perceiver makes way for liberating perception. The presence of all three of these facets marks out 'A Mind's Journey to Diss' (*CP*, p336) as a particularly useful introduction to the deeper impulses behind what Auden christened Betjeman's *topophilia*.

For this poem, written in 1968, the author drew on memories of an actual journey that he had made a few years earlier, one that resulted in a TV travelogue.[4] In both verse and film the small East Anglian town is mischievously characterised as a non-destination. In the poem, the narrator only gets as far as the railway station; in the documentary, Diss initially seems to have disappeared: Betjeman is framed staring out across empty fields from the platform as his voice-over intones dryly, 'Ah. Norfolk. Diss. Here's the station. Where's Diss?' – a classic Betjeman moment. The poem suggests that the trip to Diss, or to be more precise the thought of a future trip to Diss (as informed by the memory of a past one) was somewhat more inspirational than the reality that followed arrival. In the poem, at least, Diss looks

---

[4] *Something about Diss*, BBC, 1964, online video recording, East Anglian Film Archive, http://www.eafa.org.uk/catalogue/32 [accessed 20 January 2021].

likely to disappoint; eventually it is dismissed as 'the dimmest place of all', which reminds us that this man's excursions were made as much in the head (and in language) as they were by the body, and that the psychological need to depart and to travel was just as important as any desire to arrive. Betjeman is a poet of great expectations; even his poems of recollection are often of recalled anticipation. He also loved company, and one reason why the thought of this journey to Diss was so appealing to him is because it was to be shared: the poem was sent as a verse letter to his friend Mary Wilson, wife of then Prime Minister Harold and herself an aspiring poet. Mary was a native of Diss, and on this occasion she performs the function of significant other. Yet in a sense she is as imaginary a companion as the great big mountainous sports girl or the girl with the strongest legs in Pontefract: a reflection of the poet's need for an intimate, witnessing partner to relieve the dispiriting sense of isolation that often threatened to overwhelm him; someone he could be his enthusiastic invented self with. Less imaginary is the description of the train journey itself, which evidently draws on the poet's recollections of his earlier trip. For all his impish dissing of Diss, Betjeman – who was actually fond of the town – also pointedly instructs his viewers to remember that 'nowhere in England is dull, not even the road from that station on a wet day'. Nor evidently the less-than-scenic stretch of railway between Liverpool Street and the middle of a flat Norfolk nowhere. Retracing in his mind's eye the route that weaves first through the 'chimney-pots' of North London suburbs before heading out into the sticks, Betjeman's steadily rocking tetrameter catches the trance-inducing effects of a slow train rolling along the Great Eastern Main Line:

Flint church-towers sparkling in the light,
Black beams and weather-boarding white,
Cricket-bat willows silvery green
And elmy hills with brooks between,
Maltings and saltings, stack and quay
And, somewhere near, the grey North Sea

Is it fanciful to hear, in these linked couplets with their regular medial caesurae, the clickety-clack of bogie carriages passing over the joints in old track? Whatever, the passage offers the kind of incidental detail, recalled with evident savour and to no obvious purpose – description for its own sake – that is so characteristic of Betjeman's best topographical poetry. For dullness is in the eye of the beholder, and the beholder whose eye seeks to enlighten and entertain the world, and also to lighten his own load of cares and lose sight of his vulnerable self, finds any details that take him out of that self gratifyingly distracting.

Escaping

In the years of his fame, John Betjeman's urge to get away was partly a desire to evade the consequences of the affable accessibility that characterised his public persona. As his secretary Jill Menzies recalled, 'he'd answer every single letter and some of them from awful people sending hopeless poetry to him [...] Sometimes I could tell he was *longing* to escape and go on an outing to a church or somewhere and in the afternoon he quite often would' (*L2*, p6). Or as the much-pursued poet himself wrote, 'you can go away to Cornwall, then they discover you and you have to go somewhere else' (*L2*, p310). Yet this masks a self-motivated impulse to slip the leash that pre-dated his celebrity: 'the natural desire to escape', as Betjeman himself put it, offering this as the first reason for his trip to Australia in 1962 (*L2*, p204). This man was highly responsive to the universal urge to set off. He relished the intrinsic pleasure of travelling hopefully, although more often in Britain and Ireland than around the world, and – famously – by train rather than by plane.

Martin Jennings' much-admired statue of Betjeman on the raised concourse of St Pancras International Station depicts the poet holding onto his hat, inspecting the roof, or possibly looking for inspiration, but undoubtedly just about to depart. It's an appropriate pose. For the average commuter, time spent on a train is just an obligatory hiatus between places where the stuff of life happens; for John Betjeman, you sometimes get the impression that destinations were an obligatory termination of quality time spent on trains. Preferring stopping services partly because they extended the journey time, Betjeman was a flâneur not of boulevards but of branch lines. The inherent appeal of railway travel is something that his 'American Master' also recognised in *The Four Quartets*, although Eliot, being a sceptic, felt the need to point out the illusory nature of such 'relief': his voyagers, although 'not the same people who left that station', fail to escape from their pasts 'into different lives, or into any future'.[5] Betjeman, being a committed illusionist, revelled in the relief provided by liminal space, the intrinsic lure of the line. As he puts it in 'A Lament for Moira McCavendish', 'the roll of the railway made musing creative' for this man (*CP*, p249) – his daughter recalls that her 'mother always said he wrote most of his poems on trains'

---

[5] Eliot, 'The Dry Salvages', *Collected Poems*, p210.

(*L1*, p197) – and it's no coincidence that one of his most enraptured poems of place is 'The Metropolitan Railway' (*CP*, p169-70).

Escaping vicariously with a courting couple, here the poet imaginatively embarks from the Baker Street Station Buffet to journey back in time along a once-aspirational track. The poem opens ecstatically with the delight of anticipation, of travelling in 'radiant hope', before it pictures the rendezvous:

> Early Electric! Maybe even here
> >   They met that evening at six-fifteen
> Beneath the hearts of this electrolier
> >   And caught the first non-stop to WILLESDEN GREEN,
> Then out and on, through rural RAYNER'S LANE
> To autumn-scented Middlesex again.

In a way Betjeman is commemorating the magical world of his own conception here: the envisaged couple, having been transported by a line that was electrified in 1905, one year before the poet's birth, are about to 'conspire' for 'their children's good' (as ever, Betjeman relishes the euphemisms).[6] Zeroing in on the point of maximum incipience – before electric rails lost their shine, before rural Middlesex was engulfed by London suburbs, before the accumulating weight of experience burdened these parents-to-be – the poetry flashes like sparking points or a twinkle in the eye. Much of its delight lies in the evanescent novelty of incidental detail from the enchanted Edwardian interlude, classic Betjemaniana from a time when Art was Nouveau and Science

---

[6] Both his own parents, and those of his wife, lived close to the Metropolitan Railway during the early years of their marriages.

made the future seem bright. So here again is the electrolier; here are the arc lights which – superseding gas lamps and themselves superseded by incandescent bulbs – briefly glared over London streets around the turn of the century; and here is the smooth and safe hydraulic lift, newly installed in swanky department stores such as Oxford Street's *Selfridges*, which opened for custom in 1909. Like 'A Subaltern's Love-song', the moment of anticipatory joy caught in 'The Metropolitan Railway' is a pointedly fleeting one, and time has clearly flown by the start of the poem's final stanza, where we are bluntly informed that the young lovers have themselves been subjected to its ineluctable, corrupting influence: he has died of a malignant growth, she is suffering from a terminal heart condition. The jaunt, therefore, has the sort of gloomy destination that (as we'll see in the next chapter) so often counterpoints Betjemanic euphoria.

Hauntingly abandoned Verney Junction lay at the end of the new Metropolitan Railway line. Noting in his most-admired television documentary that suburban development never got so far, Betjeman concludes 'Grass triumphs, and I must say I'm rather glad.'[7] And here is another side to the escapee-poet's character. For as much as he relished the ornament and bustle of the station buffet, Betjeman's imagination was also drawn to marginal, sparsely inhabited spaces and to remote regions: the Isle of Man, Anglesey, the Norfolk Broads, Lincolnshire, Ireland's sleepy interior, 'dim seaside resorts' (*L2*, p376). It's as if he wanted to stretch the escape act as far as possible. More loved than anywhere else, of course, was Cornwall, England's ultimate end-

[7] *Metro-Land,* BBC, 26 February 1973.

of-the-line halt and the location of the poet's summer holidays from childhood to old age. The transformative exhilaration of getting away to this isolated, distant county is caught in a passage from 'Summoned by Bells' that travels the North Cornwall branch line aboard the express from London. As the engine passes through 'Egloskerry' and 'Tresméer' – places that sound like they belong less to an English county than a foreign country – railroad car turns into tardis, with its occupant feeling like he's been whisked off to another world, wondering if it is possible

> That this same carriage came from Waterloo?
> On Wadebridge station what a breath of sea
> Scented the Camel valley! Cornish air,
> Soft Cornish rains, and silence after steam...

> *– CP*, p418

Seaside air provides a cleansing draft to ventilate Betjeman's stanzas on more than one occasion, a breath of freedom that's contrasted to the confining and malodorous atmosphere of the City, and also to the suffocating routines and responsibilities of the daily grind. Here, as sibilance folds the engine's steam into the distinctively mild mizzle of the far south west, we're reminded again that the value of Betjeman's topographical poetry depends not on the thoughts or meditations that such places stimulate, not on ideas, but on the enchanting sense of release, and on the aesthetic attention that has been paid to the intrinsic pleasure of escape. These are lines that capture the magic of being transported, not only physically but also emotionally and imaginatively.

Company

Betjeman's topographical poems take us to places, but the psychological journey is often away from the troubled and isolated self. From boyhood jaunts around London with friend Ronald Wright in the late 1910s, through church crawls with John Piper in the middle years of the century, to a series of architectural tours with journalist Simon Jenkins in the early 1970s, John Betjeman evidently liked to do his exploring in company.[8] In his poetry, when the escape is into remembered places, it is often also into past companionship, and one senses that it's the companionship that matters most: as the poet wrote to John Sparrow, 'I am not primarily a poet of place. I never write of place first and people afterwards (at least not nowadays) but of people first and place as an inextricable part of them' (*L1*, p426). So where 'Ireland with Emily' (*CP*, pp98-99) is superficially more about the named country than the named person, devoted as it is to a loving evocation of winding bohreens and ruined demesnes, in truth it's the barely-gestured-to companion who holds the key to this poem's deeper motivation, which is the desire to salvage from the maw of time a shared memory of intimacy. Asking if the season's warmth has held, the speaker's thoughts are primarily still with his cycling partner, as he seeks to keep loneliness at arm's length through imaginatively extending their joint lease on a privileged summer:

> Has it held, the warm June weather?
> Draining shallow sea-pools dry,

---

[8] See Hillier, p28, pp516-18.

> When we bicycled together
> Down the bohreens fuchsia-high.

We can see the same thing happening when the poet goes further back into his past. The countryside of 'Norfolk' (*CP*, p168) recalls 'lost innocence' for the revisiting writer, but his wistfulness here is less for the tree-shaded lanes themselves than for what he associates with them, namely the short-lived period of peaceful intimacy between himself and his father, who he recalls showering with 'sorrel seeds' on shared walks along the rural footpaths. V.S. Pritchett has noted that 'nostalgia' in Betjeman tends to be counterpointed by a 'sense of insecurity, the terror of time and pain',[9] but in this case it is made poignant by the rift that subsequently developed between father and son, the 'unkept promises and broken hearts' that he refers to in the poem's final line. 'Trebetherick' (*CP*, pp52-3), set in Betjeman's Cornish holiday destination, seeks to revive the easy intimacies that are enjoyed in childhood through a first person plural narrative, listing those with whom the young John was on first name terms as it identifies remembered places. The supporting cast of other Cornish poems, such as 'Sunday Afternoon Service in St Enodoc Church, Cornwall' (*CP*, pp113-17), 'Beside the Seaside' (*CP*, pp128-34) and 'North Coast Recollections' (*CP*, pp135-40), is too large to credit. Sometimes, though, one special friend is all that's required. The unnamed companion of 'Hearts Together' (*CP*, p301), for example, in which Betjeman recalls another childhood holiday destination – this time on the Dorset coast –

---

[9] 'Betjeman in Pooterland', *The New Statesman*, 60 (3 December 1960), p894.

but where in truth the scenery is incidental to the innocent intimacy enjoyed by the two best buddies; or the memory of 'playmate Bobby' in 'Narcissus' (*CP*, pp280-81), a poem that begins with a topophiliac's acknowledgement that inspiration comes from an evocative location ('Bedford Park'), but goes on to concentrate on reviving a sense of the prohibited connection between the two 'bosom boyfriends' as they play hide and seek. Talking of which, as far as English poetry is concerned, there are few childhood friends more special than Wendy from 'Indoor Games near Newbury' (*CP*, pp124-25), where the superficial pleasure taken in some amusing place names ('Bussock Bottom, Tussock Wood and Windy Brake') is transcended by an intense evocation of pre-pubescent intimacy:

> Love so strong that I was frighten'd
> When you gripped my fingers tight and
> Hugging, whispered 'I'm your friend.'

If the poems of childhood places recall or envisage the kind of companionship that once had the power to keep loneliness at bay, other topographical verses see a more mature Betjeman temporarily losing himself in the personal space of others. At times these poems convey something like the vicarious closeness of the voyeur, as the poet evades isolation by getting under someone else's skin. Almost literally in 'Business Girls' (*CP*, p181) where – in a combination of lust, trains and architecture that could only have been written by one man – the eye of the observer in a carriage passing through Camden is salaciously drawn to the exposed bathrooms that jut from terraced houses that back onto the track, houses in which (the speaker fancies) the eponymous women are bathing. You sense that Betjeman's imagination has been stimulated here by a fleeting and tantalising conjunction of private and public spaces, bathrooms and carriages, the naked and the clothed; his roving poetic eye becomes an invasive force that makes short work of the houses' provocatively permeable defences. And yet I think it's significant that this intrusion leads not to fantasies of sexual possession but rather to emotional identification. Ultimately, the author is motivated more by empathy than desire in this poem. This is why the perspective switches to that of the imagined bathers gazing up through their skylights, and why the poem concludes with a narrator who seeks to soothe rather than to seize, encouraging the women to continue to take their rest in the womb-like liquid warmth. Betjeman would later depict himself in a similar position in 'Summoned by Bells', 'luxuriating' as he swishes warm bathwater around his legs (*CP*, p440), a simple pleasure that leads him to recall less happy ablutions at his school, Marlborough, 'a lonely place' (*CP*, p441). And it is the loneliness of the 'Business Girls' that he identifies with, their (assumed) condition of feeling isolated and unloved, although perhaps an element of condescension here compromises the imaginative attempt at communion. You can't look down on someone and truly occupy their space at the same time. It's a failing that Betjeman occasionally flirted with – in his depiction of a working-class North-Londoner in 'Middlesex' (*CP*, pp163-4), for example:

> Gaily into Ruislip Gardens
>   Runs the red electric train,
> With a thousand Ta's and Pardon's
>   Daintily alights Elaine.

Deferential affectation is subtly woven into this stanza through the repetition of the 'ai' sound, as this materialistic 1950s reincarnation of Tennyson's 'Elaine the fair' is associated with the concrete jungle that has displaced the still-conceivably-bucolic county of Betjeman's youth. Yet there *is* identification here. When Elaine is described as eating her sandwiches in front of the TV, we sense the empathetic impulse of the popular poet-broadcaster. Furthermore, there seems to be a genuine complexity of response when Betjeman populates his lost Elysium of Victorian Middlesex not with idealised semi-rural yokels, but disreputable young urban swells who are now long-buried. Whatever class we belong to, wherever and whenever we live, whoever's dubious company we keep, we're heading inexorably for the ultimate solitude, the poem seems to say, as it ends in Hardyesque poignancy with peppy personalities laid to rest in their gloomy graves.

Absences

We shall return to that subject, but not before a final topographical diversion. One might expect that a man subject to feelings of loneliness would find the isolated position of solitary observer an uncomfortable one, yet I've noted Betjeman's interest in end-of-the-line destinations, and he actually appears to have found a degree of solace in the description of vacant or vacated places. Whether contemplating the neglected architectural features of a seldom-visited parish church, or the flora and fauna of an empty Cornish seashore, this man evidently attained moments of inner calm by leaving the beaten track and losing himself in hitherto overlooked details. So amidst the swirling noise of the Atlantic coast's thundering waves, as recalled in 'Summoned by Bells', the poet finds that 'still and small things' of the rockpools gain significance, and that this generates a certain composure:

> Somehow the freckled cowrie would survive
> And prawns hang waiting in their watery woods;
> Deep in the noise there was a core of peace;
> Deep in my heart a warm security.

> *– CP*, pp422-23

Security was a valuable commodity for John Betjeman. Contemplative moments like this seem to be as priceless as the rare cowries, simultaneously worthless and infinitely precious. The more vividly realised and apparently purposeless the description, the more Betjeman's public persona (the entertainer and campaigner) and his private problems (the lusts and fears) fade away, and a 'core of peace' is disclosed amidst the characteristic turbulence of his emotions. 'I seek leave unimpassioned by my body', the frequently manic poet Robert Lowell once requested, and he found such respite in what he calls the 'universal' consolation of 'description without significance'.[10] Just as, in 'A Mind's Journey to Diss', Betjeman forgets himself for a passage of time in an ataractic description of a nondescript East Anglian railway corridor, so in 'Summoned by Bells' he finds temporary emotional respite by losing himself in still and small things, like the cowries, metaphors for nothing, coffers of selflessness.

Contemplation of the vacant spaces of the North Cornish coast seems to have generated several momentary escapes from the

---

[10] Lowell, 'Shifting Colours', *Day by Day* (London: Faber and Faber, 1978), pp119-20.

burden of identity like this – as the poet puts it in the first line of 'Cornish Cliffs', 'moments, tasted once and never done' (*CP*, p237). There is, for example, the meditative pause generated by a revelatory sense of deep time experienced 'By the Ninth Green, St Enodoc' (an isolated coastal golf course, *CP*, pp241-42); and the delightfully strange palimpsest of place evoked in 'Harrow-on-the-Hill' (*CP*, p148). 'Do you remember how', the poet commented in a radio broadcast, 'when one went for a holiday at the sea and then came inland, how one longed as a child to keep the sea in one's mind and keep sea-weed at home and things like that, although, all the time, one was in London?' (quoted in Peterson, p416). The poem that resulted from this memory sees location transformed, to no obvious purpose, by a writer's freely associating imagination, as he discerns the sound of surf in whispering poplar trees:

> Then Harrow-on-the-Hill's a rocky island
>   And Harrow churchyard full of sailors' graves
> And the constant click and kissing of the trolley buses hissing
>   Is the level to the Wealdstone turned to waves.

A place name's intrinsic music resounds throughout this poem as the paeon contained in 'Harrow-on-the-Hill' (a sound pattern where a strongly stressed trochee is echoed by a weaker one, as in 'melancholy') echoes down through the stanzas, reverberating across line-endings as it goes. Description is certainly revelation in this poem, as Betjeman's double exposure of Middlesex hill and Cornish harbour – a hybrid that reflects a psyche shaped by term-time experiences in London and summer holidays in the south-west – gives form to Wallace Stevens' belief that descriptive poetry should be revelatory, conjuring 'artificial' things that exist in their 'own seeming', intenser than actual life. Although an early title for the poem was 'A Child's Lament', and although Autumn may have its intrinsically melancholic qualities, I don't think that sadness is the primary emotion here. Rather, the poem conveys the wonder of serendipitous aesthetic surprise. The neurotic fears and thwarted desires that are elsewhere the hidden drivers of Betjeman's creativity have been temporarily forgotten thanks to the intrinsically pleasurable process of rhythmic re-imagination. Lost for a short space in the atmospherics of his betwixt and between dreamworld, the weight of the poet's fears and of his own isolated identity is momentarily lifted. It's an imaginative escape from the burden of selfhood similar to that which Philip Larkin achieved in his own strange and self-surprising marine meditation, 'Absences', which concludes with its narrator voicing the sense of psychological release that Betjeman leaves unsaid: 'Such attics cleared of me! Such absences!'[11]

Imaginative straying into untrespassed places occasionally enabled Betjeman to leave his anxieties and evasion tactics behind, then, but – truth be told – such aesthetic escapes from the ego were often fleeting, and not every memory of the North Cornish coast generated beguiling verse. In terms of imagery, 'Winter Seascape' (*CP*, p243-4) is probably his nearest approximation to 'Absences', its opening marked by a similarly painterly description of an elemental ocean, here cannonading against the Cornish slate and thundering into caves. Yet the iambic tetrameter of this poem

---

[11] *Philip Larkin: The Complete Poems*, ed. Archie Burnett (London: Faber and Faber, 2012) p134.

lacks the supple fluidity of Larkin's seascape (one instance where Betjeman's formal inflexibility is clearly a handicap) and it's notable that the poem's concluding stanza sees the observer reasserting his presence rather than, as Larkin does, wondering at his own absence:

> Here where the cliffs alone prevail
> I stand exultant, neutral, free,
> And from the cushion of the gale
> Behold a huge consoling sea.

There's a straining for resonance here, but it doesn't come off; in truth this constitutes a somewhat confused ending. Ostensibly, Betjeman celebrates the freedom of neutrality as his appreciation of the impersonal forces of nature releases him from a small and restrictive sense of self; yet 'exultant' and 'consoling' are not neutral terms, and suggest that this self – with its passing enthusiasms and its neediness – remains stubbornly present. Locating himself within the landscape has caused a sort of poetic camera-shake, as Betjeman's character blurs a vision that is elsewhere (in the rock pool imagery of 'Summoned by Bells', for example) sharply defined. Although it reaches a tonally opposite conclusion to this contrived moment of reassurance, something similar happens at the end of the near contemporary 'Tregardock' (*CP*, pp239-40), where an unlikely geological feature is followed by a more direct intrusion of personal insecurities:

> And I on my volcano edge
> Exposed to ridicule and hate
> Still do not dare to leap the ledge
> And smash to pieces on the slate.

Bad reviews may be unpleasant but they don't really warrant such an extreme response; confessional angst was not Betjeman's strong suit. Place and verse are also appropriated by an extraneous agenda in the last stanza of 'Dilton Marsh Halt' (*CP*, p321), which fondly anticipates the return of steam trains 'when all the horrible roads are finally done for' – a horrible line probably deserving of the same fate. There were precious moments in Betjeman's writing life when the liberating potential of an empty place, intersecting with the imaginative potential of an empty page, generated some highly therapeutic breathing space for both poet and reader. But Archie the bear would probably testify that his owner's primary remedy for loneliness was to fill the hours with work and company, notably that of his own larger-than-life invented self, and if escapades sometimes gave Betjeman the opportunity to leave this insistent persona behind, on other occasions (like Archie) it came along for the ride.

*

Responsiveness to the lure of elsewhere; the need for witnessing company; the desire to lose oneself in places and in their poetic transformation: such motivating factors reveal topographical description to be intimately linked to psychological disturbance in John Betjeman's poetry. Trains took this poet on vacations from the troubled self, but his biographer Bevis Hillier records one revealing occasion when a journey to a holiday destination brought troubling truth home to him. Journalist Simon Jenkins, one of Betjeman's many travelling companions, recalled an encounter they had at Southend Station:

We got off the train, and Betjeman was, frankly, acting. 'Ah! Wonderful place, Southend!' you see. Well, that station was ghastly. He went up to this woman and said, 'Isn't it marvellous, living in Southend, my dear? You are so lucky, living in Southend.' Anyway, she thought this man was completely crackers, and turned away and covered up her child. Betjeman was furious. He expected her to say, 'Oh, Sir John, how grateful I am ... ' but clearly she had no idea who he was.

– quoted in Hillier, p519

'Old Betje', the nation's teddy bear, was visiting the Southend of his dreams, but the real world has a habit of exposing and dispelling such fictional projections. Ultimately, reality will not be imposed upon. One anonymous woman on a platform who failed to play the game might be seen as retaliating on behalf of all of those named, unnamed and renamed women in Betjeman's poetry who were co-opted into it. In trying to evade his vulnerabilities, Betjeman – as his wife perceptively recognised – ran the risk of disappearing into his own invented persona. His reader should be wary of making a similar mistake: that is, of being so seduced or repelled by the act that the human being behind this show, whose fears, foibles and fervours give the poetry its third dimension, is completely lost to sight. Attending, finally, to some of the darker moments in this poetry allows a clearer view of features that lay beneath the entertainer's mask, although even here there's no shortage of distracting diversionary tactics.

4

MORTALITY

IN HER SELECTION OF HIS LETTERS, Betjeman's daughter Candida quotes from an article entitled 'The Lonely Laureate' in which her father confessed that he had 'sometimes [...] known such deep depression' that he wouldn't have minded something running him over (*L2*, p511). Loneliness was a source of despondency that could be temporarily alleviated by good company, whether real, imagined or stuffed, but as the years went by, it seems to have become harder for Betjeman to distract himself from the ineluctable fact of death. 'I dread the idea of extinction', the 54-year-old poet told interviewer Kenneth Allsop, 'and I think about death every day' (quoted in Hillier, p339). Religion exists partly to dispel such dread, of course, with good Christians promised – in the words of St Paul – 'that like as Christ was raised up from the dead by the glory of the Father, even so we also should walk in newness of life'. To Betjeman, it seemed that 'the only practical way to face the dreaded lonely journey into eternity' was 'the Christian one', but Paul's subsequent warning

– 'Let not sin therefore reign in your mortal body, that ye should obey it in the lusts thereof [...] for the wages of sin is death' – was less than reassuring to a man keenly aware of his own obedience to the lusts of his mortal body.[12] In 'The Conversion of St Paul' (*CP*, pp382-84) Betjeman contrasts the 'blinding light' experienced by the Evangelist to the 'fitful glow' of his own tenuous faith, one which occasionally went out altogether and consequently provided only intermittent hope in face of death. 'Almighty Saviour, had I Faith', the poet writes in 'Before the Anaesthetic' (*CP*, p108), 'there'd be no fight with kindly Death', but death is rarely characterised as kindly, or even indifferent, in John Betjeman's poetry. It is a malignant force. So where the penultimate line of 'Aldershot Crematorium' (*CP*, p302) sees the poet quoting Jesus's reassurance from the gospel of St John, 'I am the Resurrection and the Life' (*The Bible*, John 11.25), he completes the couplet and the poem not with conviction but by noting how 'doubt inserts the knife'. The image that stays with us from this piece is one of dissolution rather than resurrection: Betjeman draws attention to the smoke rising from the crematorium, the mortal remains of our beloved ones diffusing into the atmosphere.

If not often in his faith, Betjeman could find a degree of consolation in poetry. This was not an Elizabethan confidence in the enduring power of immortal lines, nor the Romantic vision of transcendence through the creative imagination; it was more

---

[12] *The Holy Bible Containing the Old and New Testaments,* Authorised King James Version (Cambridge: Cambridge University Press, 1984), Romans, 6.4; 6.12; 6.23; Betjeman, 'John Betjeman Replies' (not to St Paul), *The Spectator* (8 October, 1954), p443.

like the capacity for distraction and self-distraction that the aesthete shares with the comedian. There's no shortage of potentially gloomy subject matter in Betjeman's *Collected Poems*, yet – as he once wrote to Larkin – 'only in gloom does true humour thrive'.[13] Just as the superficial impression left by his amatory verse is of a man not seriously troubled by his own desires, his poetic approach to the ultimate source of despair is often flippant. In a tactical manoeuvre not dissimilar to making frank confessions of lust in such a way as to ensure they can't be taken seriously, the poet seeks to draw the sting of death by acknowledging it as a source of morbid fascination, whilst at the same time emasculating it through comic disdain within the structures of light verse.

In fact, Betjeman's darkly whimsical approach to the subject of mortality was one of the first things that marked out his idiosyncratic talent. 'Death in Leamington' (*CP*, pp1-2) tells the tale of an unnamed woman who passes away in a hushed bedroom:

> Beside her the lonely crochet
>   Lay patiently and unstirred,
> But the fingers that would have work'd it
>   Were dead as the spoken word.
>
> And Nurse came in with the tea-things
>   Breast high 'mid the stands and chairs –
> But Nurse was alone with her own little soul,
>   And the things were alone with theirs.

John Bayley has written perceptively about this poem, arguing

---

13 12 April 1972, British Library Betjeman Archive, Add. 71647.

that the 'somehow offensive' comedy that the poet extracts from this scene, 'in depriving it of seriousness' also confirms the poem's 'effectiveness as art' – an insight that could be applied to much of Betjeman's work. 'The world of the poem is so unusual that the platitude of death has no part in it', Bayley adds,[14] and the author certainly toys mischievously with platitudes in this ballad: the first stanza above is almost, but not quite, authentically sentimental (lonely crochet is too surreal; dead fingers are too macabre); the description of Nurse and tea-things is almost, but not quite, respectable (breasts too much in evidence). Yet if the majority of this not-quite-proper poem has its wicked way by blending 'chintzy cheeriness' with a deathbed scene, stanza six does something a little different, hinting at the poet's own wonder at the woman's apparent lack of distress at, or even awareness of, human dissolution. As he contemplates the crumbling decorative features, the peeling stucco and the plaster dropping from Italianate arches, the speaker asks, rhetorically but with genuine surprise, if the residents even realise that things fall apart and that hearts do eventually cease to beat? There is just a suggestion here that the ineluctable fact of personal entropy might seriously preoccupy the young man who is making light of it. But Leamington, where those with stiff upper lips and arthritic hips come to retire, imposes its own inflexible imperturbability onto retirement's inevitable destination. As evening calm drifts into the room, and the nurse pointlessly tiptoes away down the hall, we recognise that no one, not even the dead, should be disturbed

---

[14] Bayley, 'The Best of Betjeman', in *Selected Essays* (Cambridge: Cambridge University Press, 1984), p85.

in Royal Leamington Spa. You sense that the poet finds this not only amusing, but also incredible. As Philip Larkin would later write in his own provocative and wondering contemplation of age and personal entropy, 'The Old Fools', 'Why aren't they screaming?' (*Complete Poems*, p192)

Sometimes in Betjeman's poetry the forces of dissolution are hidden in architectural features, sometimes they are concealed by the cover of irreverent humour, sometimes they prowl just off scene, or are caught in the corner of the eye. Take, for example, 'Lord Cozens Hardy' (*CP*, pp227-8), whose chilly tomb waits in unnervingly close attendance as evanescent pleasures play themselves out in another of this poet's privileged gardens. It's still the eternal Betjeman summer – the poet's eye lingers over a 'bright East Anglian day', a children's game, more tea-things – but it also takes in the vulnerable and soon-to-be-extinguished flame of a spirit lamp, and the sepulchral darkness that lurks on the edge of the decorous activities. Imagery of ageless stone, yews, holly and oaks provides a gloomy background to the poem as watching eyes are drawn towards the 'half-seen mausoleum' that is the ancestral resting place. From the start (a mock-exclamatory 'Oh') a determinedly light narrative register has been employed to resist the gravitational pull of this *memento mori*: the poem is, after all, a ballad, and it ends in reassuring mock-horror rather than the real thing when its narrator reports the villagers' fear of encountering the deceased aristocrat on a spooky moonlit stroll. But the speaker is aware that Lord Cozens Hardy's oblivious 'children's children' are circling a plug hole. The implicit message of this poem is a universal *media vita in morte sumus*: in the midst of life we are in death.

The dead are often, in an unseemly and sometimes unnerving way, physically present and *located* in Betjeman's poetry like this. Lord Cozens Hardy waits in 'the corner of the park'; the unnamed woman lies in a stuccoed Leamington bedroom; there is also the sticky end related in 'Mortality' (*CP*, p288), where gore slips effortlessly into bathos as a senior civil servant's grey matter, reduced to 'sweetbread' due to a car accident, litters 'the corner where the by-pass | Comes into Egham out of Staines.' Not all of those whose first-class minds cease to function in Betjeman's poetry are treated quite so callously. A gentler tone characterises his sepia-tinted reflections on the death of an obscure but admired Oxford don, whose 'body waits in Pembroke College':

> Dr Ramsden cannot read *The Times* obituary to-day
>   He's dead.
> Let monographs on silk worms by other people be
>   Thrown away
>   Unread
> For he who best could understand and criticize them, he
>   Lies clay
>   In bed.
>
> – 'I.M. Walter Ramsden ob. March 26, 1947
Pembroke College, Oxford', CP, p166-67

Yet even this affectionate *in memoriam* offers the ghoulish detail of cheeks once flushed with port now drained of blood, and the short lines, in their contrast to the scholarly prolixity of the long ones, generate more black comedy than they do pathos. The same could be said about the list of shops that will no longer be receiving the custom of the housewife who now lies beneath the earth in 'Variation on a Theme by T.W. Rolleston' (*CP*, p204):

But her place is empty in the queue at the International,
  The greengrocer's queue lacks one,
So does the crowd at MacFisheries. There's no one to go to
                                                    Freeman's
  To ask if the shoes are done.

Emotional distance, if not laughter in the face of death then at least a sardonic smile, offers a psychological coping mechanism when one is confronted with the grim fact of extinction. Yet at the same time, this poet's repeated need to get up close and personal with the physical manifestations of death speaks of an underlying compulsion. No one is excluded from such post-mortem examination. It's one thing when the decaying face is that of an anonymous resident of Leamington Spa, or when the bloodless cheeks are those of an obscure fellow of Pembroke College, but – one would imagine – quite another when the grim reaper defaces your own parents. Yet even here Betjeman refuses to draw a respectful veil; by contrast, it seems that the raised emotional stakes push him to an extreme of bad taste. 'On a Portrait of a Deaf Man' (*CP*, pp79-80) – which is about the poet's father – opens respectfully enough, with its first stanza characterised by affectionate ribbing (in its description of his 'discreetly loud' tie, for example). But the macabre humour of stanzas four and seven is something else entirely:

And when he could not hear me speak
  He smiled and looked so wise
That now I do not like to think
  Of maggots in his eyes. [...]

He would have liked to say good-bye,
  Shake hands with many friends,

> In Highgate now his finger-bones
> Stick through his finger-ends.

'Is this funny? Ghastly? Horrifying?' asks Greg Morse (*Reading the Victorians*, p54). It's certainly provocative: even Bevis Hillier – no Betjephobe he – discerns an 'almost vindictive quality' in these lines (*John Betjeman*, p33). The tone is indeed an uncomfortable and contradictory one: the first half of each stanza seems authentically sentimental and speaks of filial respect, if not exactly love; the second half swings to the disrespectful extreme of brutal mock-horror. The father is part benevolent memory, part grisly revenant. His depiction is made even more unnerving by intrusions of the son's irresponsible sense of humour, about which there's something involuntary, as if Betjeman can't suppress an unsuitable scream of nervous laughter. Yet it's worth noting, I think, that the depersonalisation implicit in this poem's title reflects the fact that it isn't actually a father so much as a soulless body that arouses the poet's fascinated repugnance. It may be that this poem is being driven less by lingering Oedipal hostility than by Betjeman's need to give some dramatic expression to his own all-consuming fears, as indicated by his concluding complaint that, where God asks for belief, he sees only decay. The fact that death has come a little closer to home has prompted a more violent reaction and more extreme humour, but a corpse is a corpse is a corpse to this man, who continues to fetter his own discomfort within an essentially comedic narrative mode (and we're back in the familiar bounds of ballad meter here). 'Remorse' (*CP*, p182), where the face of death belongs to Betjeman's mother, is not much more decorous. This time the grisly image comes first:

The lungs draw in the air and rattle it out again;
The eyes revolve in their sockets and upwards stare

Again there is a shocking detachment about this, given the close relation and the moment of extremity being described; but again, this doesn't necessarily indicate personal coldness, for the soul of the individual – as the poet recognises – has departed, its absence reflected in that repeated definite article that effectively dehumanises lungs and eyes. The poet is just compelled, with a repulsed fascination, by the *actuality* of a soulless body (another thing he has in common with John Donne). Narcissistically, as in 'On a Portrait of a Deaf Man', the central issue here is less the suffering of the parent than that of the son, guilt-ridden at his own neglectful behaviour, veering uncertainly between sentimentality and the distinctly inappropriate observational humour that causes him to clock the fact that the nurse sets aside her knitting before she surveys his mother's remains.

The man who once said he thought about death every day instinctively made light of it in verse, then, yet equally felt compelled to evoke its disconcerting propinquity to life. He wouldn't wish to stroll near Lord Cozens Hardy's mausoleum, but that is where his eyes are drawn; he doesn't want to think of maggots in his dead father's eyes, yet his poetry conjures these horrors up nonetheless; the laboured breathing of his mother's final hours is the last thing he wants to hear, but it's also the last thing he invokes in his poem. Betjeman's repeated need to deny the darkness only reveals its hold on his imagination. It is notable that in none of these poems do the actual experiences of the dying feature. We are offered shocking glimpses of grim remains rather than empathetic insights into the distress, or possibly the lack of distress, of the departing human being. Perhaps contemplating ghoulish cadavers – scary but, as is emphasised in 'Remorse', beyond suffering – allowed Betjeman to give death its imaginative due yet conveniently overlook the realities of dying. When his empathetic imagination *is* more fully engaged, the afflictions of others can be sensed more clearly in poetry that becomes correspondingly both more humane and more authentically heavy-hearted.

The ironically titled 'Sun and Fun: Song of a Night-Club Proprietress' (*CP*, pp173-4) belongs in this category, offering as it does the flip side of those poems where luxury cars, country houses and seductively turned-up noses signal indulgence and escape. Where the young Subaltern sang of love blossoming in full Surrey twilight at an evening dance, the old Night-Club Proprietress sings of loves long gone in the cold light of day. The sun that once shone on exotic holidays and long weekends in country houses now barely percolates through dated, heavy curtains. Ecstacy swings to its opposite pole of despair in this poem as magical nights give way to the mundane morning after, with its unemptied ashtrays and uneaten sandwiches:

> But I'm dying now and done for,
> What on earth was all the fun for?
> For I'm old and ill and terrified and tight.

There's some empathetic feeling in those lines. Present pains are similarly juxtaposed against past pleasures in 'Devonshire Street W.1' (*CP*, p177), another ominous offering where, for one man, dancing is a distant memory and the future looks bleak.

After X-rays reveal the situation to be hopeless, his wife takes his hand as, 'loving and silly'

> At long-past Kensington dances she used to do
> 'It's cheaper to take the tube to Piccadilly
> And then we can catch a nineteen or a twenty-two.'

The disconcerting revelation of terminal illness is partially mitigated by the refuge of sentiment in this concluding stanza, which strikes a nice balance between the emotional compensations of domestic love and its evident inadequacy in face of the facts: 'silly' has inflections of both, as indeed does the wife's economising over their homeward journey. 'Inevitable' (*CP*, p230), a diagnosis poem in which Betjeman appears to draw on his visits to the sick at St Bart's hospital, portrays a similar mismatch between the pathetically vulnerable human being (who first resorts to hot-water bottles, and then to osteopathy) and the inexorable force of death. Comparing the sick man to 'a cast-off Teddy bear', the observer wonders if he might be too ill to know, or even to care, that he is dying? The questions reflect a fearful, wide-eyed curiosity about the end of life experience similar to that in 'Death in Leamington', although now it seems more pressing and personal, as physical and emotional proximity makes things increasingly urgent. There's a sense that we are getting near to the bone of Betjeman's fear now: the humour of this poem's first stanza is muted and sympathetic rather than ghoulish and inappropriate; the teddy bear is metaphorical but we can't help but visualise him as Archie, and through him, recognise the anxieties of his owner. Where Betjeman conspicuously avoids emotional involvement in the two poems about his parents, stepping in at the end to identify mortal remains and his own guilty presence instead, here he has evidently shared an anonymous stranger's final journey, developing an intimate bond of fear along the way: though both men were aware that death would soon take one of them, they struggled against it together. As a consequence, the poem's final stanza has a ring of authenticity about it that puts the nightmarish horrors elsewhere in Betjeman's oeuvre into perspective. The dying man makes one last effort to bid his companion farewell:

> His final generosity when almost insurmountable
>   The barriers and mountains he has crossed again must be.

Here the process of dying is recognised as exhausting physical labour that takes one to a remote place; death is struggled for and attained like a distant high plateau. Truly empathetic observation generates insight and a clarity of vision that ultimately – and surprisingly, given the subject matter – dispels some of the horror: this is the poet's reward for accompanying the process rather than performing some transmogrifying evasion. Yet it also has to be acknowledged that the desire to tell the truth about his experience takes some of the shine off Betjeman's poetry here. Neither particularly gloomy nor exactly glowing, 'Inevitable' sees the poet's creative engine slipping into neutral. You can't help thinking that those rhythmic polysyllables would look more at home in a lyric by W.S. Gilbert; you can't help missing that inappropriate intrusion of Betjeman's sense of humour. 'Inevitable' is more ethically admirable than aesthetically felicitous, then. For this man, poetry was primarily a means of conjuring distracting illusions, yet here is one of those situations where the need to make light has been trumped by the need to bear witness. Betjeman has reached a point where, as Eliot wrote in his own meditation on the final journey into the dark, 'the poetry does not matter' ('East Coker', *Collected Poems*, p198).

From here it's a short, funereal step to the group of poems in which the poet contemplates his own demise, and the darkness threatens to close in for good. At times the mood here is something closer to panic. In 'The Cottage Hospital' (*CP*, p178), death is not glimpsed out of the corner of the eye, nor relocated into the scary-safe realms of mock-horror; rather, it is lucidly envisioned, right down to the colour of the walls and sound of the wards, 'the tap upon polished parquet | of inflexible nurses' feet'. Envisaging himself twisting in a sweaty sheet and gasping for breath while youngsters play games outside, Betjeman's writing attains the sort of focus that signals genuine imaginative and emotional engagement: I'm thinking, for example, about the attention paid to patterns of alliteration here – onomatopoeic in the tapping feet, entwining in that twisted sheet. It's fascinating to note how such unnerving visions of expiry counterpoint the equally highly-worked and vividly-imagined fantasies of requited romance earlier in Betjeman's work, thus further emphasizing the desperation of the speaker's projected plight. At this point – when, as he puts it in 'Good-bye' (*CP*, p275), 'lust has gone out' – the kind-but-stern dominatrixes to whom Betjeman's speakers once took pleasure in submitting have nightmarishly metamorphosed into inflexible nurses, invisible reinforcers of the hospital regime; the gasps and drown'd senses of the bed of desire have been superseded by those of the deathbed. The patient in this anonymous Cottage Hospital has been terminally screened from ongoing life, yet he is only too conscious of its tantalising proximity: the insects, the playing children, those unseen nurses. He's the fly tightly shrouded in the attendant spider's web, with his imaginative suffering intensified by the fact that, as he puts it in the last two lines of the second stanza, 'none of the garden noticed | that fizzing, hopeless fight.' Eden is still there, but now it's on the other side of the window; death is conceived as a terminal ejection from the charmed garden that had once been the location of so much pleasure. Betjeman suspected that at no time are you more alone than at the point of departure, and this fear also motivates 'Five O'Clock Shadow' (*CP*, p276), another hospital poem that focuses on the horror of abandonment in 'the Men's Ward'. 'This is the time of day when we feel betrayed', whines the patient, and although there is some limited reassurance to be found in that first person plural – a camaraderie of the forsaken and condemned, which the reader is implicitly invited to join – solace is outweighed by a sense of desertion, as medics and visitors leave the stricken speaker to encroaching night. Again, bleak echoes of past pleasures are unmistakable: the dactyllic line 'Safe in her sitting-room Sister is putting her feet up', for example, offers a variation on past poetic waltzing, transferring Betjeman's favourite word to a strong woman who – far from offering protection – has withdrawn even the tap of her footsteps. There's no lime-juice and gin on offer here to take the edge off things.

Feet are mentioned several times in these later poems about mortality, and it may not be coincidental. It's a sad irony that, in old age, this poet of the dancing dactyl and the tripping trochee was also a man who was in constant fear of losing his footing. In his introduction to a 1976 book published by the Parkinson's

Disease Society, Betjeman described his condition as one of 'being unable to move your limbs at all or at least with difficulty: being unable to cross a room, let alone a street without "freezing"; being always terrified lest you fall.' (quoted in *L2,* p450-51) As it is evoked in one or two late poems, this fear had a spiritual element too. Towards the end of his life, the poet wrote to his friend the Anglican priest Harry Jarvis,

> I have a very strong feeling that this earth is going to crack beneath me and I will sink into fire through mattresses of chicken-wire, telephone cables and sewage pipes which compose the ground under our feet at Radnor. On Monday night the whole of it was bathed in an ominous pink light. Yours in the sure and certain hope of a speedy Resurrection, John B.
>
> – *L2,* p495

Ominous, ominous ... Given John B's slowed step and guilty conscience, the ironic humour of his sign-off here is very winning. 'Chelsea 1977' (*CP*, p392), Betjeman's last and most affecting poetic intimation of mortality, appeared a year later. Here the poem's deliberate, iambic steps, not to mention the difficulty with which the speaker negotiates canine deposits outside his house, are both poignant reflections of the author's growing unsteadiness. Shuffling along the pavement, his 'sense of doom' rises as he visualises the underworld just beneath his feet,

> chicken-netting coil on coil
> Covering cables, sewage-pipes and wires
> While underneath burn hell's eternal fires.

Perhaps this tangled subterranean web is partly a metaphor for the then still-hidden complexities of Betjeman's love life.

Having sold his long-abandoned family home in 1972, the poet had relocated to a new house in Chelsea, a few doors up from one owned by his second partner Elizabeth Cavendish. Whatever, there's no missing his fear of the ultimate tumble into the flames of perdition: 'chicken-netting' certainly seems less than adequate as a means to break that fall, or indeed to keep any judgemental forces that lurk below from surfacing. As all hell threatens to break loose off the King's Road, the sense of proximity and permeability between this world and the next feels both unnerving and authentic. Always good at conveying apprehensions, Betjeman here brilliantly evokes the feeling of trepidation and vulnerability that accompanies old age and frailty. But even in such gloom does true humour thrive. Finally, at the thought of 'hell's eternal fires', the dancer's instinct returns, and Betjeman's poetic feet, at least, trip briefly into the inane but reassuringly familiar and harmless world of the advertising jingles and breakfast tables of childhood:

> Snap! crackle! pop! the kiddiz know the sound
> And Satan stokes his furnace underground.

For one last time, the poet expertly catches his anxiety in the butterfly net of comedy.

*

John Betjeman was not to die harrowingly on a London pavement, or abandoned in some anonymous Men's Ward or cottage hospital, but serene and at peace on a sunny morning in his Cornish retreat, attended by his long-time 'other wife' Elizabeth, two flexible nurses Carole and Vicky, and – of course – Archie. The truth is that, to the end, he received the consideration, feminine and ursine, that he had needed throughout his life. Whether or not he's presently being roasted by hell's eternal flames remains open to question, but there is some comfort to be gleaned from Cavendish's observation that, during his final days, 'his fear of death seemed to go'.[15] Perhaps the tranquil manner of this going confirms something that Betjeman had written to Penelope nine years earlier: 'I saw a very good telly last night on hell. It was a film. It said hell is now and is separation from God. Quite true' (*L2*, p493). This man had often felt that his own flaws made that gap unbridgeable, his fear of the hereafter leading him to conclude (in 'Good-bye', another rehearsal of his own end, *CP*, p275) that – for all the futile activity – it was

> better down there in the battle
> Than here on the hill
> With Judgement or nothingness waiting me,
> Lonely and chill.

Yet the sense of separation from God closed naturally as Betjeman slipped away from his own particular hell on earth, one that had in truth been characterised less by the fire and brimstone of Hades-under-Chelsea, more by the familiar symptoms of human restlessness: anticipatory excitement and irrational trepidation; joy in company and fear of solitude; pride and self-doubt; relish of existence and dread of extinction;

---

[15] For two accounts of the poet's final hours, see Hillier, p544 and Wilson, p320.

'moments of ecstasy or depression' (*L2*, p256). In short, the stuff of poetry. During his bouts of depression Betjeman might have concurred with Edward's conclusion, in Eliot's play *The Cocktail Party*, that 'Hell is oneself' with all others 'merely projections', for 'one is always alone'.[16] But such feelings were intrinsic to the kind of poetic responses – the humorous evasions of, and more direct confrontations with, sources of distress – that, by counterbalancing his poetry of escape and wish-fulfillment, ensure that this writer will be remembered as a common sufferer as well as an exceptional entertainer.

[16] T.S. Eliot, *Collected Plays* (London: Faber and Faber, 1962), p169.

5

BETJE AMONG THE BRAINBOXES

FOR ALL THE DIVERSITY OF HIS INTERESTS and cultural output – the radio broadcasts and television appearances, the architectural journalism and guides to English counties, the endless book reviewing, the editing, the public speaking engagements, the campaigning, the committee work, and all of this and so much more – verse came first for John Betjeman. He defined himself in *Who's Who* as 'poet and hack', not the other way around. If he was insecure about many things he was always sure of his vocation: 'I knew as soon as I could read and write I That I must be a poet', as he asserts in 'Summoned by Bells' (*CP*, p408). What he was less certain about was whether or not he was a good one. As A.N. Wilson has emphasised, and like many a writer before him (his beloved Tennyson springs to mind), this man had an almost pathological sensitivity to any form of perceived disparagement (see *John Betjeman*, pp4-5). 'Our poems are part of ourselves,' Betjeman wrote in 1971, 'they are our children and we do not like them to be made public fools of by strangers' (*CH*, p383). The most popular English poet in living memory feared and loathed critics and suspected that it was only a matter of time before they would expose him as a fraud rather than the 'real thing'. The director of *Metro-land*, Eddie Mirzoeff, recalls being struck by Betjeman's sense that his success 'was a temporary phenomenon, that he was in vogue and therefore able to scratch a living, but that it wouldn't last and that he would unquestionably end in the workhouse. He used to say that regularly as a joke – but it was one of those things that you knew *wasn't* a joke' (quoted in Hillier, p470). The joke that isn't really a joke: that distinguishing feature of Betjeman's poetry. His popularity was near its zenith when, following the publication of the *Collected Poems*, the poet advised his publisher, with sardonic pessimism, that there would 'be the reaction' and that he would 'suffer contempt, neglect and frustration' (ibid., p377). And so it came to pass.

Fearful of the critics and doubting his own capabilities, Betjeman's favoured strategy in the war of reputations was a quintessentially English one: making light of his own particular talents became one of his main talents; he sought to charm and disarm through humorous self-deprecation, both in interviews ('I don't think I am any good', as he confided to a reporter from *The Times* following his appointment as Poet Laureate) and in the poems themselves.[1] The doggerel apology for a verse preface in his last volume *High and Low* is typical. Betjeman attempts to spike the guns of his reviewers here by contrasting the products of his 'plastic pen' to the immortal lines of notables from John Murray's back catalogue, asking how 'a buzzing insubstantial fly'

---

[1] Tim Devlin, 'Sir John Betjeman, the New Poet Laureate: Summoned by Success', *The Times* (11 October 1972, p16).

like him could emulate such luminaries? 'I do not try' (*CP*, p235), he concludes, and if you don't try no one can say that you have failed. Elsewhere, as we have seen, creative failure and critical rejection are themselves occluded by the poetry, becoming a source of comedy in – for example – 'Summoned by Bells', a poem that more than one critic was to reject as a creative failure. Betjeman inoculated his work with the vaccine of self-mockery in the vain hope that it would be immunised against more virulent evaluative forces that were beyond his control.

In fact, there has never been a shortage of the charmed and disarmed amongst common readers and fellow writers, and Betjeman *has* also had notable champions within the universities – fellow Johns Bayley, Gross and Carey, for example, have all written perceptively on his distinctive qualities (see Hillier, p437, p484). But as far as Academia in general is concerned, Betjeman's poetry has long been regarded as a familiar folly that warrants the occasional passing comment but no detailed investigation, worthy of an article or chapter maybe, but rarely a monograph. His corpus waits patiently for attention just off-stage, the Lord Cozens Hardy of English Literature. 'Summoned by Bells' indicates that the neglectful disdain of university readers was one source of Betjeman's defensiveness and self-doubt. His declaration of vocation in the second part of this poem is immediately followed by a reference to the centre of learning that was, at time of writing, still associated with the cutting evaluative (more often devaluative) criticism and cultural elitism of F.R. Leavis. 'Even today', Betjeman writes,

> When all the way from Cambridge comes a wind
> To blow the lamps out every time they're lit,
> I know that I must light mine up again.
>
> *– CP*, p408

Having once been cast to the winds by another centre of learning,[2] Betjeman retained a dim view of judgemental academics: 'I could hardly expect the approval of these poor accentless, rootless, joyless brain-boxes', was his defensive response to the mixed reviews of his verse autobiography (quoted in Hillier, p399). Self-deprecation was balanced by defiance, then. When Betjeman relights the anachronistic lamp of his creative endeavour, he's fully aware that he is offering precisely the kind of obsolete metaphor that, in the eyes of many a New Critic, debarred him from serious consideration altogether. Moments of calculated contrariness like this are easy to misread as simple incompetence.

It could be argued, then, that the uncertainty of this writer's reputation within the higher educational system was born as much out of mutual incompatibility as out of the poetry's intrinsic shortcomings. Betjeman and Academia enjoyed the briefest of relationships, but separated at an early stage due to irreconcilable differences: the poet who 'could not *think'* felt alienated by the cogitations of the 'brain-boxes'; the critic who was paid for serious explication, when confronted by Betjeman's frivolous and self-explanatory stanzas, felt at a loss for words. 'One cannot imagine a *Student's Guide* to Betjeman's *Collected Poems'*, wrote Patrick

---

[2] He was actually awarded a pass degree from Oxford University (that is, a degree without honours), an ignominious success less appealing to his sense of humour than ironic failure.

Taylor-Martin in 1983, before going on to argue that he failed to satisfy the academic 'lust for difficulty', affording professional poetry analysts 'no opportunity to show off; no occasion for a dazzling display of erudition or ingenuity with which to impress colleagues and rivals and thereby secure academic preferment' (*John Betjeman - His Life and Work*, p180). Well, the culture of Higher Education has clearly changed since Taylor-Martin's book was published, and Betjeman, like a long-neglected stock, may be ripe for some speculative attention; Greg Morse's appreciative study of his extensive debt to the Victorians has since filled one research niche, and indicates the possibility of a wider reconciliation. Yet however much one would like to agree with Morse's prediction that 'the tides have started to turn' in Betjeman's favour, the 'three in-depth books on the poet' (p6) that he cites as evidence – given the accelerating metastasis in academic publishing since Betjeman's death in 1984 – still look like exceptions that prove a continuing rule of neglect. Thus far attempts to accommodate this writer within the sophisticated discourses favoured by contemporary university English studies – such as, for example, Morse's own tentative characterisation of Betjeman as, perhaps, 'the ultimate postmodern pioneer?', or Brown's description of his technique 'as incipiently "postmodern" in the terms that Jean-Francois Lyotard has laid down' – sound more than a little forced.[3] You can see the poet rolling his smiley gloomy eyes.

If the academic 'neglect' of his verses can be put down to the fact that old Betje and the new lecturers speak different languages,

---

[3] Morse, *Reading the Victorians*, p188; Brown, *John Betjeman*, p12.

then other factors lie behind the element of 'contempt' that the poet also anticipated. I hope that this reassessment has shown that there's more to Betjeman's poetry than is evident at first glance, be that admiring or dismissive, but whether this is nice more or nasty more is another question. When you survey negative responses to this writer, you occasionally sense something more hostile than objective evaluation. Even an appreciator like Carey, when reviewing instalments of Hillier's biography, felt the need to itemise Betjeman's character flaws: 'vindictive, snobbish and disloyal', 'exploitative, querulous, calculating and deceitful'.[4] There is often a perceptible aversion to the *man*, occasionally the 'ridicule and hate' that the poet himself describes in 'Tregardock' (p240). The list of Betjephobes – for example, Geoffrey Grigson, John Wain, Al Alvarez, Ian Hamilton, Tom Paulin, Ian Sansom – spans the generations, and there's more than a hint of something personal about their critical objections, as if Betjeman's very status as 'poet' offends sensibilities. As is often the case in Britain, verbal attacks sometimes imply simmering class resentment, although in truth this is more often than not an internecine struggle within the middle class – a broad church 'riddled with subtle distinctions', as the poet himself recognised.[5] When Sansom, reviewing the second volume of Hillier's monumental biography, rather brutally awarded Betjeman the status of 'dead English minor poet', he was making a value judgement that cannot be wholly disassociated from his wickedly memorable characterisation of said poet as 'a

[4] Carey, 'A talent to abuse', review of Hillier, *John Betjeman: New Fame, New Love, Sunday Times* (3 November 2002, p33).

[5] 'Bedford Park, Chiswick', *Betjeman's Britain,* p269.

silly little man with a taste for posh totty'.[6] It may be that what Sansom describes as this writer's 'high regard for anyone with a title' (ibid.) has contributed towards his blacklisting in egalitarian critical circles. Of course, it could be said in response that Betjeman also had a high regard for many people without titles, and that the inverted snobbery of his detractors is equally problematic and self-deluding. J. Betjeman, the son of a man 'in trade' who aspired to aristocratic ease (yet, in practice, worked his socks off all his adult life – he rarely turned down job offers, and as his popularity grew his schedule became punishing), offends the sensibilities of A. Critic, who's probably employed in an instructor's role by an educational institution, does occasional reviewing, and prefers to align himself with the labourers. I also notice that I've thoughtlessly masculinised A. Critic, and that my list of Betjeman detractors is exclusively male, a disparity that, in this case, does not necessarily indicate the existence of an unacknowledged legion of female fans ... There's a feminist study of this poetry waiting to be written, but given the roles into which Betjeman casts women, it's unlikely to be complimentary. Perhaps most damaging of all, though, in a society that has become increasingly aware of the extent to which the young and vulnerable have been subjected to exploitation by male authority figures, is the sense that – for all their comic exaggeration – Betjeman's erotic projections still reflect and foster the kind of unhealthy sexual objectification that fuels potentially hazardous masculine fantasies. The 'confident girl prefect' of 'A Russell Flint' may herself

[6] Sansom, 'Happy Knack', review of Bevis Hillier, *John Betjeman: New Fame, New Love, London Review of Books,* 25.4 (20 February 2003), pp27-8.

be a figure of authority, and 'Myfanwy' a 'chum to the weak' and emasculated male (*CP*, p277, p70), but our difficulty imagining a contemporary incarnation of such schoolgirl muses tells us something about the dramatic change in social mores since Betjeman's mid-twentieth-century heyday. There *are* good reasons why this poet has fallen out of fashion.

As we've seen, John Betjeman certainly had his flaws and foibles, some concealed, some candidly admitted. When his empathetic imagination fails him, as it did increasingly in his later years, he can caricature individuals in a distinctly reductive manner: not only the clichéd 'Woman Driver' (*CP*, p386) and the 'Civilized Women' (*CP*, p389), but also the raging male driver of 'Meditation on the A30' (*CP*, p285) and the uncivilized 'County' Porkers (*CP*, pp316-18). Alongside sexism and snobbery, the poet himself acknowledged (in 'Guilt') that he wore a 'breastplate of self-righteousness | And shoes of smugness' (*CP*, p365), and occasionally his poetic feet look similarly cossetted; some evocations of leisured, privileged existence can just seem trivially self-satisfied ('Seaside Golf', with its 'glorious, sailing, bounding drive' and concluding vision of 'splendour, splendour everywhere' springs to mind, *CP*, p165). If the snobbery and smugness had been deep-rooted, though, the bestowal of honours – the knighthood in 1969 and elevation to the status of Poet Laureate in 1972 – might have encouraged such flaws to flourish and express themselves effusively in more forgettable verse. Yet in practice a sense of obligation to the establishment completely extinguished this writer's capricious, incorruptible creative spark – a rather painful but edifying irony for a dedicated social climber. In fact, the slightest hint of pomposity and dutifulness, such as in the few 'official' poems that he felt compelled as Laureate to write in commemoration of significant royal occasions, instantly dispels the charm that, in his poetry as in his social life, this poet so assiduously sought to weave. That Betjeman's poetic skills invariably failed to rise to the occasional can be taken as a mark of his integrity. When he tried to be good he was usually bad; when he trifled he could be a lot of fun. He knew this well enough. 'I don't think I am any good', the defensively self-deprecating Poet Laureate told *The Times* in 1972, but having disarmed his interrogator, his subsequent comment – 'and if I thought I was any good I wouldn't be any good' – reveals a canny appreciation that one of his particular strengths lay in an awareness of his own limitations, in not taking himself too seriously. Betjeman made light not only of genuine concerns, but also of his own unique capabilities.

Having said that, the insouciance that first seduces Betjeman's more sympathetic readers does not, in itself, provide sufficient evidence on which to base a convincing case for the revaluation of his much-patronised poetry. Its worthiness (and the poet will be turning in his grave at that word) as a subject of attention ultimately depends on its capacity to detain as well as to entertain us. And for that, for a meaningful relationship to be established between writing and reader, we need to feel that the poems have a dimension beyond their superficial appeal. It doesn't have to be a hidden complexity of ideas or concepts; it's enough when we sense the presence of a real human being behind the projected persona. Just as the revelation of routinely concealed insecurities and character flaws can make us warm to someone rather than be repelled by them, so it is that this author's vulnerabilities, whether they lurk in the depths or bubble up to disturb the surface of the verse, contribute significantly to his emotional claim on us.

And with this in mind, back to Archie. When he contemplated why we should be able to accept John Betjeman's teddy bear 'when we want to stuff Sebastian Flyte's down his throat', Philip Larkin concluded that 'no doubt sincerity is the answer, a sincerity as unselfconscious as it is absolute'.[7] It's a problematic assertion, given that self-conscious affectation was built into Betjeman's poetic DNA. Yet, as we have seen, his was an affectation complicated by the disconcerting sense that his tongue might not, after all, be in his cheek. Perhaps, on a deeper level, we respond because we consistently sense that the relish of personal pleasures and irresponsibility so characteristic of Betjeman's verse does not exclude – indeed, is born out of – the recognition and experience of personal fears and emotional burdens, ones that, ultimately, are universal. 'My themes,' said John Betjeman, 'are that you're all alone, that you fall in love, that you've got to die.' Buddhists would understand these as symptomatic of the three poisons that afflict us all – delusion, attachment and aversion – and their concomitant emotions – loneliness, craving and fear. In this context, delusion is identification with the ego or self-image, which generates the misapprehension that we somehow stand separate from the rest of the universe, and results in a sense of ineluctable solitude. Falling in love appears to provide one remedy for this

---

[7] Larkin, 'The Blending of Betjeman', review of *Summoned by Bells,* reprinted in *Required Writing* (London: Faber and Faber, 1983), pp129-133, p132.

perceived isolation, as the ego seeks to confirm its existence through identifying an elusive soulmate or missing other half. But becoming attached to egoic projections invariably results in disappointment, as reality stubbornly refuses to match our ideal template. The ego would also seek to elude the most basic, anxiety-inducing truth of all: that of impermanence, of our own physical mortality. Betjeman's more pithy summary of the things that keep us from enlightenment could be seen as an astute spiritual self-diagnosis, then, indicating awareness of his own intense susceptibility to such provocations. Delusion, craving and aversion generated strong creative responses in this man, and poetry that negotiated these things offered a (short-lived) antidote to the poisons that often ran through his veins. For this relief Betjeman was intensely appreciative: 'I know nothing in the world, not even love, quite as fulfilling as completing a poem to one's satisfaction', he once told his daughter (quoted in Hillier, p435). Given his susceptibility to 'love', that was saying something. It may be that the excessive mood swings that characterised both Betjeman's life and his writing mark an emotional and spiritual immaturity that meant contentment was always going to elude this man. Unlike Denis Brown, I'm not at all convinced that he was one who faced 'the world and his deepest fears with a degree of equanimity' (*John Betjeman*, p63). If his poetry is anything to go by, John Betjeman was not good at maintaining equilibrium. But in his very susceptibility to fears and responsiveness to desires, we recognise him as essentially one of us, albeit writ large; and in his ability to transform stress into aesthetic elegance, to shed some light on the darkness, we should find something to admire. We're prepared to accept Archie, with his one smiley eye and his one gloomy eye, because – like the poetry – he reflects a sensibility that could encompass both the frivolous and the serious, the desire for adventure and the need for security, the urge towards sensual excess that generates its own guilts and counterbalancing movement towards spiritual atonement. The bear who was, according to his keeper, 'very interested in Temperance Work at Clacton-on-Sea' (*L1*, p79) was also the bear whose owner's daughter once found in a somewhat disreputable state:

> One morning I remember getting back to the Mead at about eleven o'clock, and finding the doors locked and arrows painted on card pointing towards the lawn. There, sitting beside the goldfish pond, was JB's teddy bear Archie holding an empty whisky bottle, surrounded by several other empty spirit bottles.
>
> – *L2*, p52

Giving full rein to the delights of self-indulgence, yet also betraying the desire for abstinence that springs from a guilty conscience, John Betjeman's poetry bears compelling witness to the intoxicating and distressing condition of being an unenlightened human.

SELECT BIBLIOGRAPHY

By the Poet: Writing

Betjeman, John. *Collected Poems.* Introduction by Andrew Motion. London: John Murray, 2006.

_____ *First and Last Loves.* London: John Murray, 1952.

_____ *Betjeman's Britain.* Edited by Candida Lycett Green. London: The Folio Society, 1999.

_____ *Betjeman's England.* Edited by Stephen Games. London: John Murray, 2010.

_____ *Coming Home: An Anthology of Prose.* Edited by Candida Lycett Green. London: Methuen, 1997.

_____ *Letters: Volume 1 1926-1951.* Edited by Candida Lycett Green. London: John Murray, 1994.

_____ *Letters: Volume 2 1952-1984.* Edited by Candida Lycett Green. London: John Murray, 1994.

_____ *Betjeman on Faith: An anthology of his religious prose.* Edited by Kevin J. Gardner. London: SPCK, 2011.

_____ *Tennis whites and teacakes.* Edited by Stephen Games. London: John Murray, 2008.

By the Poet: Broadcasts

_____ *Trains and Buttered Toast: Selected Radio Talks.* Edited by Stephen Games. London: John Murray, 2006.

_____ *Sweet songs of Zion: Selected Radio Talks.* Edited by Stephen Games. London: Hodder & Stoughton, 2007.

_____ 'John Betjeman goes by Train: King's Lynn to Hunstanton'. British Transport Films, 1962.

_____ 'Larkin and Betjeman: Down Cemetery Road'. Monitor series. BBC1, 15 December 1964.

_____ 'Metro-land, with John Betjeman'. Produced by Edward Mirzoeff. BBC1, 26 February 1973.

_____ 'Something about Diss', BBC1, 1964.

_____ 'Time with Betjeman'. Seven programmes. Produced by Jonathan Stedall. BBC2, 1982-3.

About the Poet

John Bayley, 'The Best of Betjeman'. *London Review of Books,* Vol. 2 No. 24, 18 December 1980.

Jocelyn Brooke, *Ronald Firbank and John Betjeman,* Writers and their Work series. London: Longmans, Green and Company, 1962.

Dennis Brown, *John Betjeman.* Writers and their Work series. Plymouth: Northcote House, 1999.

Bevis Hillier, *John Betjeman: The Biography.* Abridged edition. London: John Murray, 2006.

Philip Larkin, 'The Blending of Betjeman'. *Required Writing.* London: Faber and Faber, 1983.

Greg Morse, *John Betjeman: Reading the Victorians.* Brighton: Sussex Academic Press, 2008.

Seamus Perry, 'Betjeman's Tennyson'. *Tennyson Among the Poets.* Edited by Seamus Perry and Robert Douglas-Fairhurst. Oxford: Oxford University Press, 2009.

William S. Peterson, *John Betjeman: a Bibliography.* Oxford: Clarendon Press, 2006.

Patrick Taylor-Martin, *John Betjeman: His Life and Work.* London: Allen Lane, 1983.

A.N. Wilson, *Betjeman.* London: Hutchinson, 2006.